Inspirational Basketball GOATS Stories, Amazing Facts, and Trivia Games

THE ULTIMATE BASKETBALL BOOK FOR CHILDREN AND TEENS!

Harris Baker

Contents

Introduction   V

The Legendary Basketball Heroes Biographies !

    Steph Curry   3

    Shaquille O'Neal   12

    LeBron James   18

    Kareem Abdul-Jabbar   25

    Magic Johnson   32

    Larry Bird   38

    Bill Russell   45

    Wilt Chamberlain   51

    Tim Duncan   57

    Kobe Bryant   63

    Michael Jordan   69

Amazing Facts, Records, and Moments

    Epic Basketball Blunders   77

    Dunk Legends: Gravity-Defying Feats   80

    Hoops in Space: Galactic Basketball Adventures 83

    Mascot Mayhem: The Wildest Court Mascots   86

    Animal Invasions: When Wildlife Takes the Court 89

    Ancient Hoops: Historic Games that Shaped Basketball 91

    The Hidden Stars of Basketball   94

Odd Rituals and Lucky Charms   97

Cutting-Edge Basketball Innovations   99

Basketball Brain Games And Trivia!

Game 1 - Basketball Rules Trivia Challenge   103

Game 2 - Spot the Difference: Historic NBA Finals   106

Game 3 - Basketball Legends Word Search   108

Game 4 - Basketball Math Challenge   110

Game 5 - Basketball Timeline: Evolution of the Game   112

Game 6 - Fill-in-the-Blanks   114

Game 7 - Pattern Recognition: NBA Draft Picks and Rookie   116
Achievements

Solutions - Basketball Brain Games And Trivia!

Game 1 - Basketball Rules Trivia Challenge (Solution)   120

Game 2 - Spot the Difference: Historic NBA Finals (Solution) 122

Game 3 - Basketball Legends Word Search (Solution)   124

Game 4 - Basketball Math Challenge (Solution)   125

Game 5 - Basketball Timeline (Solution)   128

Game 6 - Game 6 - Fill-in-the-Blanks (Solution)   130

Game 7 - Pattern Recognition: NBA Draft Picks and Rookie   132
Achievements (Solution)

Afterword   133

Introduction

Hey there, future hoop stars. Welcome to the ultimate basketball adventure! Whether you're just learning to dribble or dreaming of sinking game-winning shots, this book is for you.

Get ready to meet some of the coolest legends in basketball history—like Michael Jordan, LeBron James, and Steph Curry. These players can light up the court and leave everyone in awe. But that's just the start. We're diving into some fun facts, wildest moments ever, from epic dunks to animal cameos on the court (yep, that really happened!).

And because we know you love a challenge, we've packed in some fun games and puzzles. Think you know everything about basketball? Let's see if you can ace our trivia, spot the differences, and more.

Oh, and before you dive in, here's a little secret: just ***Scan*** the QR code below and subscribe to our giveaways! You could win awesome free books, and more!

Lace up your kicks, and let's get started. You're about to have a slam-dunk of a time!

Harris Baker

The Legendary Basketball Heroes Biographies !

Steph Curry

FROM BABY-FACED PLAYER TO OLYMPIC CHAMPION

Steph Curry's story kicks off in a land filled with basketballs, baby bottles, and probably very tiny high-tops. In 1988, in Akron, Ohio, Dell and Sonya welcomed a baby whose future was so bright it practically needed sunglasses. Dell Curry, an NBA sharpshooter with a legendary stroke, already had game. But nobody, not even Dell, could've predicted his son would become the human cheat code we now know as Steph Curry.

If you're curious why Steph was born in Akron—a place best known as LeBron James's hometown—that's because Dell was playing for the Cleveland Cavaliers then. So, you could say Steph was born where basketball swished through the air like destiny. As the first-born Curry child, Steph got the full VIP treatment. This wasn't a kid growing up not knowing a jump shot from a jelly sandwich; he was practically bottle-fed basketballs. Instead of cooing "mama," he was probably murmuring "splash." But before those epic shots and records, let's talk about how it all began.

With an NBA player for a dad, you're bound to pick up a few tricks before you can walk properly. Dell took Steph to practices and games, where baby Curry soaked up the atmosphere like a sponge in a water balloon fight. Imagine little Steph, eyes wide, watching giants toss the ball around, dreaming of the day he could do it too—even if dribbling looked more like an awkward waddle.

The Curry family moved to Charlotte, North Carolina, where Dell spent most of his career with the Hornets. Here, young Steph began to take shape—like a basketball version of Play-Doh molding into something special. With Dell's mentorship and Sonya's athletic genes (she was a volleyball star), Steph was destined for the court. He grew up with a basketball in one hand and a bowl of cereal in the other—which might explain his slick handle from years of balancing breakfast while dribbling. In the Curry household, there were probably more basketball drills than chores.

By elementary school, Steph was already showing signs of being a basketball whiz. While other kids were figuring out how to tie their shoes, Steph was sinking three-pointers on a Fisher-Price hoop. Don't let that baby face fool you; he was all business when it came to basketball. His parents didn't have to push him into the sport—he was sprinting toward it with the kind of enthusiasm most kids reserve for candy. One key moment was when he started playing in his local youth league. Youth basketball is typically a chaotic mix of kids unsure which basket is theirs, but for Steph, it was his natural habitat. Smaller than most kids, what he lacked in height, he made up for in skill and that quick-release jumper that would become his trademark.

Steph's childhood nickname was "Baby-Faced Assassin," which might sound extreme for a kid who hadn't lost all his baby teeth yet, but it fit. He had the precision and cool demeanor that would leave defenders scratching their heads and asking, "How did he do that?" It was like he had a secret weapon hidden in that innocent smile—a jumper so pure it could've been bottled as the world's smoothest beverage. Soon, Steph became the talk of Charlotte. His dad's NBA buddies started noticing, with someone always pointing at Steph saying, "That kid's going to be special." It might sound cliché, but with Steph, it felt like destiny. He had the skills, the drive, and most importantly, the relentless work ethic that set him apart.

Yet, Steph wasn't the most intimidating presence on the court. Smaller than his peers, he didn't rely on raw power. Instead, he developed a basketball IQ that was off the charts. Always thinking two steps ahead, he outsmarted opponents with skill, speed, and sheer cleverness that had adults shaking their heads in disbelief. As years passed, Steph continued to hone his craft. He spent hours practicing his shot, even when friends were off playing video games or, you know, being regular kids. He made the impossible look routine, turning his small frame into an asset. And he did it with a smile that could melt the ice in a Gatorade cooler.

By high school, Steph had a dream and wasn't about to let anything stand in his way. Still small but playing with the confidence of someone twice his size, it didn't matter that he couldn't dunk or was undersized. What mattered was that when he had the ball, magic happened. His shot was smoother than butter on a hot pancake, and his handles were so tight. Steph Curry was on a mission, and he was just warming up.

As Steph entered his teenage years, he faced the crossroads every young athlete knows—the moment when raw talent meets real competition. The little boy content with shooting hoops on his Fisher-Price rim was now entering the jungle of high school basketball. This was where the legend of Steph Curry really began to take shape.

He enrolled at Charlotte Christian School and quickly became a standout. But let's not kid ourselves—things weren't smooth sailing from the start. Still smaller than most peers, his skinny frame didn't scream "future NBA superstar." He looked more like he'd lead the debate team than a fast break. But Steph never let doubters get to him. While other kids his age were figuring out what they wanted to be, Steph was already working on his craft like a mad scientist obsessed with the perfect formula.

Imagine being at a high school game. Players are tall, athletic, clearly built for this. Then there's Steph—looking like he could get knocked over by a strong gust of wind. But the moment the ball touches his hands, something incredible happens. His handles are so smooth you'd think the ball was glued to his palm, and when he shoots, it's like watching a magician—you never get tired of it because it's always nothing but net.

As a freshman, barely hitting 5-foot-7, Steph wasn't filling out his jersey like a power forward. But where others relied on muscle, Steph sharpened his skills to a razor's edge. He couldn't outmuscle opponents, so he outsmarted them. His coach, Shonn Brown, saw something special in the scrawny kid with the baby face and devastating jump shot. Despite plenty of doubters, Coach Brown believed in Steph's potential. High school basketball is full of kids who can jump out of the gym, but rare to find one with Steph's intelligence and craftiness. His basketball IQ was off the charts.

Steph had to prove himself against players who were bigger and stronger. Yet, every time he stepped onto the court, he delivered. He might've looked like he'd get picked last in gym class, but in reality, he was the kid you wished was on your team. He wasn't just playing basketball—he was putting on a clinic. By sophomore year, Steph had grown—to about 5-foot-9—not a giant, but his game had matured in ways stats couldn't capture. He wasn't the fastest, but he was quick. Not the strongest, but tough. Most importantly, he was deadly from beyond the arc. Give him an inch, and he'd drain a three-pointer before you could blink. His shot was like a heat-seeking missile.

High school games became spectacles when Steph was on the floor. People came not to see the team but to see what Steph Curry would do next. Pull up from half-court? Break someone's ankles with a nasty crossover? Steph played with effortless grace that made everything look easy—almost too easy. But behind that ease was incredible work. Steph wasn't just practicing; he was obsessively refining every detail. Whether his shooting form, dribbling, or court vision, he was always looking to improve.

One big challenge was gaining the attention of college scouts. You'd think with his skills, recruiters would line up, but he was overlooked by many big schools. Colleges wanted big, strong, flashy players. Steph, with his lean build and unassuming demeanor, didn't fit that mold. But instead of getting discouraged, he used this as fuel. He wasn't going to let recruiters define his future.

Then, in what can be described as a stroke of good fortune, Davidson College came calling. Not a basketball giant, but Coach Bob McKillop saw in Steph what others missed. He didn't care that Steph wasn't a physical specimen; he cared that the kid could flat-out play. With a scholarship offer, Steph made the decision that would change everything.

When Steph graduated from Charlotte Christian, he'd grown into a leader. His senior year was filled with highlights that made jaws drop and left opponents shaking their heads. Steph had something special—something beyond height or weight. He had the heart of a champion, the mind of a basketball genius, and a shooting touch that was simply magical.

Steph's high school journey was about overcoming obstacles, proving doubters wrong, and setting the stage for a career that would redefine basketball. At this point, nobody could've predicted what was next. All they knew was that this kid from Charlotte was heading to Davidson with a chip on his shoulder and a burning desire to make his mark.

When Steph Curry arrived at Davidson College in 2006, he was an under-the-radar recruit. Davidson wasn't a basketball factory; it was more like a cozy bakery, serving up solid teams with a pinch of success now and then. But that was about to change. Steph Curry was about to turn this quaint school into the epicenter of college basketball—even if nobody knew it yet.

From the moment he laced up for the Wildcats, there was something special. Here was this skinny kid, barely 160 pounds, who looked more like he was auditioning for a coming-of-age movie than taking on college basketball. But when Steph had the ball, it was like watching a magician eager to reveal his next trick. Not the fastest or tallest, but with undeniable magic that made everyone stop and stare.

Coach Bob McKillop had taken a gamble on Steph, and it paid off quickly. Steph became the team's go-to guy, not by overpowering opponents but by outthinking and outplaying them. His first season was a revelation. As a freshman, he averaged 21.5 points per game, breaking the NCAA freshman record for three-pointers with 122. Yes—122 three-pointers. He was practically raining threes like he had a vendetta against the rim. But it wasn't just about numbers. Steph played with fearlessness. He didn't care who was guarding him—some 6'8" giant or a seasoned veteran—he was getting his shot off, and it was going in. He wasn't shooting from right under the basket either. He was pulling up from ridiculous distances, the arc on his shot so high it seemed to brush the rafters before swishing through the net.

By his sophomore year, word spread that something special was brewing at Davidson. The Wildcats were no longer just a scrappy team; they were becoming a legitimate threat, and Steph was the reason. He was electrifying, combining sharpshooting with skill and creativity that made him nearly unstoppable. But it wasn't until the 2008 NCAA Tournament that he became a household name.

The 2008 NCAA Tournament—March Madness—is where Steph went from a secret to a national sensation. Davidson entered as a 10th seed, expected to be just decent. But with Steph leading, "decent" was redefined. In the first round against Gonzaga, most had written off Davidson. Steph lit up Gonzaga for 40 points, single-handedly carrying Davidson to an 82-76 victory. He was hitting shots from everywhere—threes, mid-range, layups. The Gonzaga defense looked stuck in slow motion while Steph moved with the grace of a maestro. That game was Steph's way of saying, "Hello, world! I'm here!"

Steph wasn't content with one spectacular performance. In the second round against Georgetown, a defensive powerhouse, Steph scored 30 points, leading Davidson to a 74-70 victory. People started believing Davidson could make a deep run. Next was Wisconsin, another tough defense. Steph poured in 33 points as Davidson cruised to a 73-56 victory, advancing to the Elite Eight. That's right—the Elite Eight. Davidson, a school most hadn't heard of, was now on the brink of the Final Four, and the entire country was captivated by this underdog story led by a skinny kid rewriting the game's rules.

The Cinderella run ended in the Elite Eight against Kansas, a team loaded with future NBA talent. Even in defeat, Steph shone brightly, scoring 25 points. Kansas eked out a 59-57 victory. Davidson's run was over, but Steph's star had only begun to rise. He'd scored 128 points in four games, averaging 32 points per game, solidifying his status as March Madness's breakout star.

After that tournament, there was no going back. Steph returned to Davidson for his junior year, continuing to dazzle and leading the nation in scoring with 28.6 points per game. He wasn't a flash in the pan; he was the real deal. His range was limitless, his basketball IQ sky-high, and his ability to take over a game unparalleled.

Despite his success, Steph remained grounded. He didn't let the hype get to his head, staying focused on his game and team. The same humble, hardworking kid who'd been overlooked in high school was now on the cusp of something extraordinary. Steph's time at Davidson was ending, but he'd already left an indelible mark on college basketball, transforming a small school into a giant-killer and turning himself into a superstar.

With college behind him, Steph set his sights on the NBA. In 2009, he entered the NBA Draft with dreams as big as a kid finding a golden ticket in a chocolate bar. But, as always, the path wasn't straightforward. Despite his heroics, scouts doubted him—too small, too slight, not athletic enough. But if we've learned anything, doubters only fuel Steph's fire.

The Golden State Warriors saw what others overlooked and grabbed him with the seventh overall pick. From his first NBA game, Steph began redefining what's possible. His rookie season had ups and downs, with flashes of brilliance amid injuries and adjustments. Behind the scenes, he was working tirelessly, honing his craft like a blacksmith forging a legendary sword.

Early in his career, Steph faced challenges. Persistent ankle injuries threatened to derail his dreams. Surgeries, rehab, endless training became his new normal. But Steph didn't just bounce back—he bounced higher. He transformed weaknesses into strengths, strengthening his body and refining his game to levels that left the basketball world in awe.

By the 2012-2013 season, the world got a taste of what was coming. Steph started lighting up scoreboards like a kid who'd found cheat codes to his favorite video game. He set a new NBA record for three-pointers in a season with 272 makes, leaving defenders and fans in disbelief. And that was just the appetizer.

Over the next few years, Steph didn't just play basketball; he revolutionized it. His ability to drain threes from anywhere forced teams to rethink defenses. Coaches who once focused on protecting the paint scrambled to guard a player who could score from the parking lot. Steph turned the three-pointer from a specialty weapon into a primary attack, stretching defenses thinner than string cheese.

In 2015, Steph led the Warriors to their first NBA championship in 40 years, capturing the MVP award. His dazzling plays and infectious enthusiasm ignited a basketball revolution, inspiring a new generation to embrace the long-range shot. The following year, he outdid himself, becoming the first unanimous MVP in NBA history, shattering his own three-point record with 402 makes. The Warriors set a new record with 73 wins.

But it wasn't all smooth sailing. The Warriors suffered a heartbreaking loss in the 2016 NBA Finals after leading the series 3-1. Instead of wallowing, Steph and the team came back stronger, adding superstar Kevin Durant. They claimed back-to-back championships in 2017 and 2018, with Steph continuing to dazzle. His ability to overcome adversity and elevate his game became a hallmark of his career. In 2021, Steph continued pushing boundaries. He became the NBA's all-time leader in three-pointers made, surpassing Ray Allen. His influence on basketball culture was such that kids everywhere started hoisting up deep threes, shouting "Curry!" as they let the ball fly.

Steph also embraced his role as a leader and role model. He used his platform to make a difference, launching the Stephen and Ayesha Curry Foundation to support education, health, and wellness initiatives. Known for his humility, work ethic, and commitment to family, he endeared himself to fans.

Steph Curry's basketball journey, already filled with records, championships, and mind-bending moments, reached a new peak in summer 2024. After a career defined by game-winning shots and changing the way the game is played, Curry finally added one piece of hardware that had eluded him: an Olympic gold medal. And not just any gold medal—this one came in city of lights, Paris, where Curry put on a show for the ages, capping off a legendary run with a performance that will be talked about for generations.

Curry had never competed in the Olympics before 2024. Shocking as it seems, the player who conquered nearly every challenge hadn't donned the red, white, and blue on the sport's biggest international stage. But when the Paris Olympics came, Steph joined a roster with NBA legends like LeBron and Durant—all united under Team USA.

Global competition was fierce, with teams like France, Serbia, and Brazil featuring NBA talent eager to take down the Americans. But with Steph, Team USA had an ace—someone who could pull off the spectacular when needed most. As the tournament progressed, it was clear this wasn't going to be easy. Team USA faced tough tests, including a nail-biting semifinal against Serbia, where they clawed back from a 17-point deficit. In that game, Curry's clutch shooting ignited the comeback, reminding everyone why he's one of the greatest. His calm under pressure, hitting threes from ridiculous distances, was the difference between going home early and advancing to the final.

The gold medal game was against host nation France. The atmosphere in Bercy Arena was electric, with French fans filling the stands. France, led by the towering Victor Wembanyama, was determined to upset the American giants. But Curry had other plans. From the tip-off, he controlled the tempo, threading passes, slicing through defense, and, of course, draining three-pointers with surgical precision.

The game was tight, with France staying within striking distance. Each time the USA tried to pull away, France clawed back. But in the final minutes, when pressure was highest, Steph stepped up. With Team USA's lead cut to three points and the French crowd on edge, Curry delivered four devastating three-pointers in quick succession. Each shot felt like a dagger, silencing the arena and crushing French hopes. By the final buzzer, Curry had 24 points, with eight of his twelve field goals from beyond the arc.

As confetti fell and players embraced, this victory was special. For Curry, completing the ultimate basketball journey was soul-stirring. With a gold medal around his neck, he stood at the pinnacle of his career, having conquered every challenge the sport offered. His performance in Paris was a fitting climax to a story that began on humble courts in Charlotte and took him to the very top of the basketball world. He showed that skill, precision, and relentless dedication could triumph over doubts and stereotypes. He proved you didn't have to be the tallest or strongest to make a monumental impact—you just had to put in the work and believe in yourself.

Shaquille O'Neal

one Man, Many Names, Endless Impact

We're about to embark on a whirlwind ride through the early life of the one and only Shaquille O'Neal, a towering figure who has become the legend known as "The Diesel" or "Superman". Long before Shaq was a global superstar, a four-time NBA champion, and a 15-time All-Star, he was a kid with big dreams and an even bigger frame, growing up in places that never expected to host a future Hall of Famer!

Shaq was born in 1972, in Newark, NJ, a city famous for its robust culture and rich history. Born to Lucille and Joe, Shaq's early family life was complicated. Joe faced some tough times when Shaq was a baby, which meant Shaq's mom, had to take care of him mostly by herself until she met and married Army sergeant Phillip Harrison. Shaq's early years in Newark were full of unique experiences that shaped the person he'd become later.

Imagine being in fifth grade and seeing someone who could easily be mistaken for a high school senior—that was Shaq. By the time he was 10, he was already over six feet tall, an imposing figure who commanded attention wherever he went. He was the kind of kid who stood out not just for his height but for his lively personality and mischievous sense of humor. His stepfather, Philip, was a career Army sergeant, which meant the O'Neal family moved around quite a bit, living on military bases across the globe. From Newark, they moved to bases in Germany and later settled in San Antonio, Texas. It was during his time in Wildflecken, Germany, that Shaq began to take basketball seriously. He played for the local team on base and honed his skills, finding solace and structure in the game amidst all the moving around. If there was a gym and a hoop, young Shaquille was there, working tirelessly on his craft, dunking on anything in sight!

In fact, in one of the more legendary anecdotes of his youth, Shaq shattered backboards with such regularity that local gym owners started to dread his arrival. During a high school game in Germany, he famously broke a backboard, causing the entire hoop to collapse, which earned him a reputation as a force of nature on the court. Imagine a towering, yet immensely agile teenager, soaring through the air, and then—CRASH!—there goes another backboard. The term "Shaq-proof" hadn't been coined yet, but gymnasiums quickly learned to reinforce their equipment when he was around.

Shaq's high school career took off when his family settled in San Antonio, TX. Standing at 7 feet tall by his senior year, he led his team to a 68-1 record over two years, culminating in a state championship in 1989. Yes, you read that right, 68 wins and only 1 loss! His presence on the court was like having an NBA star in a high school league. He averaged 32 points, 22 rebounds, and eight blocks per game during his senior year. Opponents probably felt like they were playing against a tank with sneakers. He could score, rebound, block shots, and even handle the ball like someone much smaller, occasionally leading fast breaks and dishing out assists. His coaches and teammates often joked that it was unfair for other teams. One legendary story from those days involved a particularly unlucky rival player who dared to take a charge against him. Now, taking a charge against a normal high school player is brave, but taking a charge against a young Shaquille O'Neal? That's borderline reckless. The poor kid ended up sprawled out on the floor, staring up at the ceiling, probably wondering if he'd been hit by a runaway freight train.

Alongside the dunk contests and shattered backboards, he was also known for his infectious personality and his ability to make people laugh. Even as a teenager, he had an unforgettable presence, filled with jokes, pranks, and a sense of humor that made him a favorite among his friends and coaches. His charisma was evident early on and would become one of his defining traits throughout his life. Shaq's high school dominance earned him a scholarship to Louisiana State University (LSU), where he played under coach Dale Brown, who already met Shaq years earlier during his time in Germany, where he recognized the young giant's potential. At LSU, Shaq's legend would only continue to grow. He was a two-time All-American, two-time SEC Player of the Year, and received the Adolph Rupp Trophy as NCAA men's basketball player of the year in 1991. He averaged 21.6 points, 13.5 rebounds, and 4.6 blocks per game over his college career.

When the Orlando Magic selected Shaquille O'Neal as the first overall pick in the 1992 NBA Draft, the basketball world was abuzz with excitement. The Magic, a pretty new team that started in 1989, were looking for a cornerstone player, and they found it in Shaq. Everyone knew the league was about to undergo a transformation as soon as he shook hands with NBA Commissioner David Stern. In addition to his 7-foot-1, 325-pound frame and immense talent, Shaq had an air of personality and entertainment value that the NBA had rarely seen in a big man. He was poised to be not just a dominant player but also a marketable superstar who could elevate the league's profile.

He had an outstanding rookie season, quickly living up to the hype. In his debut game in 1992, against the Miami Heat, O'Neal scored 12 points, pulled down 18 rebounds, and blocked three shots, leading the Magic to a 110-100 victory. Not only were his numbers astounding, but so was the way he controlled the floor, altering shots, commanding double teams, and energizing his teammates. He became the first rookie to be named an All-Star starter since Michael Jordan in 1985. Shaq was smashing records and, quite literally, backboards. During one especially powerful dunk in Phoenix in 1993, Shaq threw down a slam that caused the entire hydraulic system supporting the basket to collapse, resulting in a 20-minute delay. There hadn't been such a display of raw power since Darryl Dawkins' famous backboard-shattering dunks in the 1970s.

Shaq was named the 1993 NBA Rookie of the Year, capturing 96.2% of the votes, after averaging 23.4 points, 13.9 rebounds, and 3.5 blocks per game during his rookie campaign. Additionally, he was selected as a starter for the All-Star Game, becoming the first rookie center to start in an All-Star Game since Kareem Abdul-Jabbar in 1970. He had an amazing ability to combine tremendous physical strength with the agility and dexterity of smaller players, often leading fast breaks and showcasing his ball-handling skills. He was setting new standards for what a big guy could accomplish in basketball, surpassing the typical role of a center who simply played near the basket.

Shaq's influence, though, extended well beyond his on-court activities. His off-court persona shined with vibrant energy and a penchant for entertainment. In 1993, he released his debut rap album 'Shaq Diesel,' which went platinum—a rare feat for athletes-turned-musicians. He also ventured into acting, appearing in movies such as 'Blue Chips' (1994) and later starring in 'Kazaam' (1996). His ability to transform press conferences into moments of stand-up comedy and provide memorable soundbites that matched his impressive dunks was remarkable. He coined phrases, gave himself nicknames like "The Big Aristotle," and kept everyone entertained.

One of the most important years for Shaq and the Magic was the 1994–1995 NBA season. With the addition of Anfernee "Penny" Hardaway, whom the Magic acquired in a draft-day trade in 1993, the team became one of the most dynamic young squads in the league. Shaq and Penny formed a formidable duo, blending size, speed, and skill. With a 57-25 record at the end of that season, the Magic secured the best record in the Eastern Conference. Shaq averaged 29.3 points, 11.4 rebounds, and 2.4 blocks per game that season. For the first time in franchise history, the team advanced to the finals, defeating the legendary Michael Jordan and the Chicago Bulls in the Eastern Conference Semifinals, and then the Indiana Pacers in the Conference Finals. Though the Houston Rockets, led by Hakeem Olajuwon, eventually swept them in four games, the message was evident: Shaq was a formidable opponent, and the Magic were a rising force in the NBA.

While he was a member of Orlando, Shaq continued to refine his game. He led the league in scoring during the 1994–1995 season and was a perennial All-Star selection. There was no denying his presence in the paint; he was a dominant force offensively and a rim protector defensively. Few players could equal his ability to influence the game on both sides of the court. Off the court, he fostered a warm and often humorous relationship with the Orlando community and its supporters. Shaq seemed to have a heart as big as his 22 shoe size, whether he was purchasing toys for neighborhood kids around the holidays, visiting children's hospitals, or cracking jokes with fans during signing sessions. He embraced his role as a community leader and used his platform to give back.

The NBA's world shifted in 1996 when Shaquille left the Orlando Magic to join the Los Angeles Lakers. His departure was one of the most significant moves in NBA history, signaling a new era for both franchises. The Lakers, already steeped in championship history from the days of Magic Johnson and Kareem Abdul-Jabbar, provided the ideal platform for Shaq's ambitions and exuberant attitude. His decision was influenced by many things: the allure of Los Angeles, opportunities in entertainment, and a $121 million contract over seven years. Shaq was switching jerseys not just to change teams but to declare his plan to dominate the NBA and chase that coveted championship ring.

Expectations were high for the Shaq era in Los Angeles, but the first few seasons under coach Del Harris fell short of championship caliber. Despite assembling a talented roster, including the up-and-coming Kobe Bryant, the Lakers were eliminated in the playoffs each year, failing to reach the NBA Finals. In 1999, Phil Jackson—the "Zen Master" himself, renowned for leading the Chicago Bulls to six titles—entered the picture as head coach. Jackson brought with him the triangle offense, a system designed to maximize team efficiency through spacing, ball movement, and player roles. This offense was perfectly suited to fully utilize the skills of each of his players—especially Shaq, who developed into an unstoppable force at the center of the Lakers' strategic triangle. Under Jackson's guidance, the Lakers began to coalesce into a championship-caliber team.

The pivotal season was 1999–2000. Every game that Shaq played was a reflection of his career peak. He dominated the league, winning the NBA Most Valuable Player award with an astounding average of 29.7 points, 13.6 rebounds, 3.8 assists, and 3.0 blocks per game. He was also named the NBA All-Star Game MVP and was selected to the All-NBA

First Team and the All-Defensive Second Team, completing one of the most decorated seasons for a single player in NBA history. More significantly, though, Shaq guided the Lakers through the playoffs and into the NBA Finals, where they faced the Indiana Pacers. Shaq's Lakers won the series in six games, demonstrating their utter dominance. He was named the Finals MVP, averaging 38 points and 16.7 rebounds per game in the series. His 43 points and 19 rebounds in Game 1 set the tone for the series and remain one of the most memorable performances in Finals history. This championship was Shaq's first and the Lakers' first since 1988.

The Lakers went on to win three straight titles from 2000 to 2002, completing a rare "three-peat." Shaq's supremacy throughout this time was evident; he was chosen Finals MVP each time, becoming only the second player after Michael Jordan to win the award three consecutive times. His and Kobe Bryant's collaboration turned into one of the most productive duos in basketball history. Despite some rocky moments and personal tensions, their on-court chemistry lifted the Lakers to unprecedented heights. Shaq and Kobe's partnership was a study in contrasts: Kobe's surgical accuracy, relentless work ethic, and intense competitiveness paired with Shaq's overwhelming physicality, dominant presence in the paint, and cheerful personality. Together, they were unstoppable!

Shaq's significant impact continued to spread. Fans and the media alike loved him for his lighthearted nature. He continued his musical pursuits, releasing additional rap albums like 'Shaq Fu: Da Return' and 'You Can't Stop the Reign,' collaborating with artists such as Notorious B.I.G. Shaq also expanded his acting career with roles in films like 'Kazaam' and 'Steel'. He made numerous guest appearances on television shows and became a regular pitchman for major brands, further cementing his status as a pop culture icon. His appeal and charm exemplified the growing crossover between sports and entertainment, and he leveraged his fame to become one of the most marketable athletes in the world.

Even though they won a lot, Shaq and Kobe didn't always get along because they had different ideas about leading and working. The tension reached a boiling point during the 2003–2004 season, culminating in the Lakers' loss to the Detroit Pistons in the NBA Finals. In a significant shake-up, Shaq was traded to the Miami Heat in July 2004. But in the annals of NBA history, his tenure with the Lakers remains a brilliant period marked by dominance and excellence. Shaq was more than just a player in Los Angeles; he was a sensation, a figure who brought joy, amazement, and three championships to the star-loving city. His impact on the Lakers' legacy and the NBA as a whole is indelible.

LeBron James

HOMETOWN HERO, GLOBAL ICON

Let's buckle up for the wild ride of LeBron James' life. Our story starts in the bustling city of Akron, OH, where in 1984, a future basketball legend was born. But hold your horses, we're not diving into his NBA days yet. We're rewinding way back to the days when little LeBron was no taller than your kitchen counter.

LeBron James entered the world with a powerful cry, probably echoing like a game-winning buzzer-beater in the delivery room. His mother, Gloria, was only 16 at the time. Raising LeBron on her own, she faced many challenges, but their bond was unbreakable.

Growing up, LeBron moved around frequently, bouncing from one apartment to another due to financial struggles. Imagine having more addresses than pairs of sneakers! Sometimes, life was tough, and LeBron even missed school because of the constant moving. Yet, despite that, basketball was his steadfast companion. When he was nine, a local youth football coach named Frank Walker introduced him to organized basketball. Even before he could properly tie his shoelaces, he was dribbling around like he owned the playground. It was as if the basketball hoop and the ball were magnetic and LeBron, the human force of nature, was destined to be caught in between.

Fast forward to school days, LeBron attended St. Vincent-St. Mary High School, a small Catholic school in Akron. This wasn't a big flashy school with a top-tier basketball program. But boy, did it get a surprise package with LeBron and his close friends Sian Cotton, Dru Joyce III, and Willie McGee—they were known as the "Fab Four." The first time he stepped on the court, it was obvious that something special was brewing. In his freshman year, he led the Fighting Irish to a perfect 27–0 record and a Division III state title, averaging a jaw-dropping 18 points per game. This kid could score from anywhere on the court—downtown threes, mid-range jumpers, acrobatic layups—you name it. It wasn't long before the whole town, and eventually the whole nation, took notice.

LeBron's sophomore year saw him shine brighter. He averaged 25.2 points and 7.2 rebounds per game, leading his team to another state championship. He became the first sophomore ever named Ohio's "Mr. Basketball" and was selected to the USA Today All-USA First Team. The media, always hungry for the next big thing, flocked to see this prodigy. Reporters were running around, trying to get a glimpse of the high school phenom. The gym was packed every game, and if you were late, tough luck—you'd end up standing on tiptoes behind three rows of people.

In his junior year, things hit fever pitch. LeBron was on the cover of "Sports Illustrated," with the headline reading "The Chosen One." Imagine being 17 and having a major sports magazine anoint you as the future of basketball—that's like being told in high school that you're going to be the President—no pressure, right? He averaged 29 points, 8.3 rebounds, and 5.7 assists per game, and was named Gatorade National Player of the Year. His team won their third state title, and LeBron was solidifying his place as the top high school player in the country.

LeBron's senior year was like a victory lap. By this time, he was a national sensation. His games were broadcast on ESPN2, and scouts from every major NBA team were drooling over his potential. He averaged an astounding 31.6 points, 9.6 rebounds, and 4.6 assists per game, often flirting with triple-doubles. This high schooler was putting up numbers that seasoned professionals would envy. Still, there were obstacles along the way. LeBron faced immense pressure and scrutiny, including a brief suspension for accepting throwback jerseys as gifts, which raised questions about his amateur status. There were debates and discussions about whether he should skip college and head straight to the NBA. Critics questioned if he was ready for the big leagues, while fans eagerly awaited his every move. Through it all, LeBron remained cool and composed, handling the spotlight with the finesse of a seasoned pro. From humble beginnings in Akron to becoming the most talked-about teenager in the country, his journey was filled with highlights, challenges, and an unwavering determination to succeed. And this, my friends, is where our tale begins—with a young boy who dared to dream big and played even bigger.

From the bright lights of high school gyms to the dazzling arenas of the NBA, LeBron James' journey was just getting started. By the time he declared for the NBA Draft in 2003, the anticipation was palpable. It was like waiting for the latest superhero movie to hit theaters, and everyone knew LeBron was about to become a blockbuster. The Cleveland Cavaliers, holding the first overall pick, made the most obvious choice in the history of obvious choices. With the first pick of the 2003 NBA Draft, they selected LeBron James. Hometown hero stays home—it was a Cinderella story from the get-go, but instead of glass slippers, LeBron was lacing up Nike sneakers.

As he donned his Cavaliers jersey with the number 23, there was a sense that something special was brewing in Cleveland. His debut in 2003, against the Sacramento Kings was a spectacle. He dropped 25 points, grabbed 6 rebounds, and dished out 9 assists—the best debut performance for a prep-to-pro player. Watching LeBron play, you'd think the basketball was part of him, like a superhero with a trusty gadget.

LeBron's rookie season was a whirlwind. He averaged 20.9 points, 5.5 rebounds, and 5.9 assists per game—a stat line that had veteran players raising their eyebrows. He became the youngest player to score 40 points in a game and was named the NBA Rookie of the Year, becoming the first Cavalier to earn the honor. The excitement around LeBron was like a rocket soaring upward, and the world was watching him climb. But it wasn't all slam dunks and highlight reels. LeBron faced the relentless grind of the NBA season, and the Cavaliers didn't have the strongest roster. They struggled, finishing the season with a 35–47 record. It was clear that while LeBron was a phenom, basketball was still a team sport, and he needed more support around him.

In his second season, he became the youngest player in NBA history to record a triple-double, showcasing his versatility and proving he was more than just a scorer. His averages jumped to 27.2 points, 7.4 rebounds, and 7.2 assists per game. Despite his monumental efforts and earning a spot on the All-NBA Second Team, the Cavaliers missed the playoffs again, but the promise of what could be was undeniable.

The 2005–2006 season marked a turning point. LeBron made his first NBA All-Star appearance, scoring 29 points and earning the All-Star Game MVP award. The Cavaliers, under his leadership, made it to the playoffs for the first time since 1998. It was as if Cleveland was waking up from a long basketball hibernation, and LeBron was their prince charming. The playoffs, however, were a different beast. In his first postseason, LeBron faced the Washington Wizards in a thrilling first-round series. He averaged nearly 35.7 points per game, including a game-winning layup in Game 5, leading the Cavaliers to a hard-fought victory. The next challenge was the Detroit Pistons, a well-oiled machine known for their stifling defense. Despite LeBron's heroics, including averaging over 26 points per game, the Cavaliers fell in seven games. It was a bitter pill to swallow, but the taste of playoff basketball only made LeBron hungrier.

LeBron's early NBA career was marked by rapid growth and a relentless pursuit of greatness. The 2006–2007 season saw him pushing boundaries once again. He led the Cavaliers to a 50–32 record and back into the playoffs. This time, LeBron was determined to take them further. In the Eastern Conference Finals against the Pistons, LeBron delivered one of the most memorable performances in NBA history. In Game 5, with the series tied 2–2, he scored the Cavaliers' final 25 points and 29 of their last 30 in a double-overtime victory. It was a display of dominance that left everyone in awe. The Cavaliers eventually won the series and advanced to the NBA Finals for the first time in franchise history.

The Finals, however, were a harsh reality check. Facing the seasoned San Antonio Spurs, the Cavaliers were swept in four games. LeBron, though magnificent, was up against a team with more experience and depth. It was a humbling experience, but one that steeled his resolve. He averaged 22 points, 7 rebounds, and 6.8 assists in the Finals, respectable numbers but not enough against the Spurs' formidable lineup.

LeBron's early years in the NBA were a blend of breathtaking performances, learning curves, and a constant drive to improve. His ability to adapt, grow, and lead was evident from the start. Each season, he added new dimensions to his game, preparing for the moment when he could lift the ultimate prize.

LeBron James' journey through the NBA landscape was akin to a thrilling saga filled with electrifying highs and dramatic challenges. As the 2007–2008 season unfolded, LeBron was no longer the fresh-faced rookie; he was evolving into a formidable force, carrying the Cavaliers on his broad shoulders with each passing game. That season witnessed LeBron not merely playing basketball but orchestrating a symphony of skills and strategy. He led the league in scoring, averaging a staggering 30 points per game, showcasing an arsenal of moves that left defenders scrambling like kids chasing an ice cream truck. However, despite his Herculean efforts, the Cavaliers were eliminated in the second round of the playoffs by the Boston Celtics, a team stacked with talent and experience.

LeBron's tenure with the Cavaliers was marked by his pursuit of excellence, yet the ultimate prize, an NBA Championship, remained elusive. The 2008–2009 season was another testament to his abilities. LeBron earned his first NBA MVP award, averaging 28.4 points, 7.6 rebounds, and 7.2 assists per game. Under his leadership, the Cavaliers secured the best regular-season record in the league at 66–16, but their playoff run was cut short in the Eastern Conference Finals by the Orlando Magic. Despite averaging 38.5 points in the series, the frustration of falling short fueled LeBron's determination even further. The 2009–2010 season followed and saw LeBron capturing his second consecutive MVP award. His performances were filled with gravity-defying dunks, no-look passes, and clutch plays. The Cavaliers once again had the best regular-season record. Yet, they faced disappointment in the playoffs, this time bowing out to the Celtics in the second round. The weight of carrying a team on his own was becoming apparent, and LeBron began contemplating his future.

Then came "The Decision." In a move that shook the NBA world to its core, LeBron announced in a nationally televised special that he was taking his talents to South Beach to join the Miami Heat. This decision ignited a whirlwind of reactions, from burning jerseys in Cleveland to jubilant celebrations in Miami. LeBron, Dwyane Wade, and Chris Bosh formed a superteam, setting their sights on championships with the fervor of kids eyeing the biggest prize at a carnival.

LeBron's first season with the Heat was a rollercoaster. The team faced immense scrutiny and pressure, with every game dissected by analysts and fans alike. Despite a rocky 9–8 start, the Heat found their rhythm and stormed through the playoffs, reaching the NBA Finals. However, the Dallas Mavericks, led by the indomitable Dirk Nowitzki, proved too much, and the Heat fell in six games. The loss was a bitter pill, and LeBron faced criticism unlike anything he had encountered before, particularly for his underwhelming performance in the Finals.

But true to his nature, LeBron used the setback as fuel. The 2011–2012 season saw a more focused and determined LeBron. He added new facets to his game, improving his post play and refining his defense under the guidance of Hall of Famer Hakeem Olajuwon. The season was shortened due to a lockout, but the Heat once again marched to the NBA Finals, this time facing the young and dynamic Oklahoma City Thunder. LeBron was unstoppable, averaging 28.6 points, 10.2 rebounds, and 7.4 assists per game in the series, leading the Heat to victory and clinching his first NBA Championship. He was named Finals MVP, overcoming the setbacks of the previous year's loss.

With the championship monkey off his back, LeBron's confidence soared. The 2012–2013 season was a masterclass in dominance. The Heat went on a 27-game winning streak, the second-longest in NBA history. LeBron won his fourth MVP award, becoming one of only a few players to achieve this feat. The Heat returned to the NBA Finals, facing the San Antonio Spurs. In a grueling seven-game series, LeBron's brilliance shone through, culminating in a Game 7 performance where he scored 37 points and secured his second consecutive championship and Finals MVP.

The 2013–2014 season was a test of endurance and resilience. The Heat reached the NBA Finals for the fourth straight year but were overpowered by the Spurs in a rematch, losing in five games. Despite the loss, LeBron's legacy in Miami was cemented with two championships and countless unforgettable moments.

In the summer of 2014, LeBron made another monumental decision—he announced he was returning to Cleveland. The prodigal son was coming home, driven by the desire to deliver a championship to his beloved Ohio. The Cavaliers, now featuring rising star Kyrie Irving and newly acquired Kevin Love, were instant contenders. The 2014–2015 season was filled with promise, but it was not without challenges. Injuries to key players in the playoffs tested the Cavaliers' depth and resilience. LeBron carried the team to the NBA Finals, where they faced the Golden State Warriors. Despite his heroic efforts, averaging 35.8 points, 13.3 rebounds, and 8.8 assists, the Cavaliers fell in six games.

But LeBron's story was far from over. The 2015–2016 season was a testament to perseverance and redemption. The Cavaliers dominated the Eastern Conference, setting up another Finals clash with the Warriors, who had set a record with 73 regular-season wins. Down 3–1 in the series, all hope seemed lost, but LeBron delivered performances for the ages, including back-to-back 41-point games in Games 5 and 6. In Game 7, with the score tied in the final minutes, LeBron executed "The Block" on Andre Iguodala, a play that became legendary. He secured a triple-double, and the Cavaliers won 93–89, completing the greatest comeback in NBA Finals history. LeBron was named Finals MVP, delivering Cleveland its first major sports title in over 50 years.

LeBron's road to stardom was a journey of resilience, evolution, and relentless pursuit of greatness. His ability to rise above challenges, adapt his game, and lead with unwavering determination cemented his place among the basketball elite. Each chapter of his career was a testament to his extraordinary talent and unyielding spirit—a legacy that continues to inspire and captivate.

Kareem Abdul-Jabbar

THE TOWER FROM POWER

Before Kareem Abdul-Jabbar soared above NBA courts, he was a baby named Ferdinand Lewis Alcindor Jr., making his grand entrance into the world in Harlem, New York City, in 1947. Harlem then was the heartbeat of African-American culture—a symphony of jazz notes, vibrant art, and community spirit. Now, when most babies make their debut, they're cute and cuddly; Little Lew—as everyone called him—was a bit more... substantial. Tipping the scales at a whopping 12 pounds and stretching 22.5 inches long, he was practically dunking over the other newborns in the nursery! It's as if the universe whispered, "This one's destined for greatness."

As Lew grew up in the 1950s, he was literally above the height curve. At 9 years old, he stood at 5'8", towering over his teachers and even giving streetlights a run for their money! Navigating a world designed for shorter folks, he sometimes felt like a friendly giant among Lilliputians. Harlem's streets were alive with the soulful tunes of Duke Ellington and Miles Davis, the air thick with creativity and the scent of possibility. The local playgrounds, echoing with the rhythmic bounce of basketballs, became Lew's favorite stage—his own personal theater where he could stretch both his legs and his dreams.

Surprisingly, young Lew didn't initially set his sights on hoops. He fancied himself the next Jackie Robinson, dreaming of smacking home runs out of the park. But when you're taller than the outfield fence by age ten, swinging a bat gets a tad awkward! His dad, Ferdinand Sr., was a transit cop by day and a smooth trombone player by night—a regular superhero with a jazz soundtrack. His mom, Cora, kept things running smoothly as a department store price checker, making sure no one got away with a bargain they didn't deserve. Together, they instilled in Lew the virtues of education, humility, and hard work—ingredients for success whether you're hitting homers or shooting skyhooks.

At St. Jude's Parish School, Lew was as much a giant in the classroom as he was on the playground. An avid reader, he devoured books like they were snacks, munching through tales of history, science, and far-off lands. His teachers marveled at his curiosity—it's not every day you meet a kid who can discuss the fall of the Roman Empire before recess! Despite standing out (literally), Lew was gentle and a bit shy, more likely to be found buried in a book than basking in the limelight. After all, it's hard to hide when you're the tallest kid in school, but Lew managed to keep a low profile—well, as low as 5'8" can be.

Life took a slam-dunk turn when Lew enrolled at Power Memorial Academy—a place where books were thick, and the basketball program was even thicker. Under the watchful eye of Coach Jack Donohue, basketball transformed from a casual pastime into a fine art. Donohue was the kind of coaches that molds players; he was crafting maestros of the court. He drilled Lew on the essentials: footwork as precise as a dance, shooting mechanics smoother than jazz, defense that could make opponents question their career choices, and above all, the essence of teamwork and sportsmanship. Lew's agility was mind-boggling for someone who could probably touch the moon on his tiptoes. He trained relentlessly, polishing his skills until they shone brighter than a new pair of sneakers.

Lew didn't just make an impact at Power Memorial—he caused a basketball revolution. Leading the team to a jaw-dropping 71-game winning streak, he turned victory into a well-worn habit. They snagged three consecutive New York City Catholic championships and clinched the national high school championship in 1964. His on-court dominance earned him the nickname "The Tower from Power," which sounds like a superhero—and let's be honest, he pretty much was. Racking up 2,067 points and 2,002 rebounds, he pulverized records. Opposing teams tried everything short of tying his shoelaces together to stop him, but Lew was a one-man wrecking crew.

Off the hardwood, Lew was as grounded as a well-rooted tree. He and his dad would spend hours soaking in jazz records, letting the smooth melodies of Miles Davis and John Coltrane wash over them. Music was a family tradition. The turbulent winds of the 1960s didn't escape his notice either. Inspired by giants like Martin Luther King Jr. and Malcolm X, Lew became deeply invested in civil rights issues. The era's fight against racial inequality was the backdrop of his formative years, shaping his worldview and stoking a fire for justice that burned as brightly as his passion for basketball.

As high school wrapped up, Lew found himself more popular than the latest dance craze. College recruiters swarmed like bees to honey, each offering a golden ticket to their institution. The University of Michigan, St. John's, Boston College—they all wanted a piece of "The Tower from Power." But after much deliberation (and probably a few coin tosses), Lew set his sights on sunny California, choosing UCLA. The allure wasn't just the palm trees and beaches; it was Coach John Wooden, a man who didn't only rack up wins but crafted champions on and off the court. Wooden's "Pyramid of Success" was a life manual that clicked with Lew's own values like puzzle pieces.

Touching down in Los Angeles in 1965, Lew stepped into a world that felt like it was in Technicolor. Gone were the towering brownstones of Harlem, replaced by sprawling campuses, palm trees swaying like they didn't have a care in the world, and sunshine that seemed to last forever. It was like stepping into a postcard. NCAA rules, being the fun police they sometimes are, barred freshmen from varsity play, so Lew took his talents to the freshman squad. But don't think for a second that slowed him down. In a scrimmage that had more hype than a Hollywood blockbuster, Lew led the freshman team to a resounding victory over the varsity squad—the same varsity squad that had just clinched the national championship! Talk about stealing the show.

When Lew finally donned the varsity jersey in 1966, college basketball braced itself. Standing at a towering 7'2" and moving with the grace of a gazelle, he was the kind of player coaches have nightmares about. Enter the skyhook—Lew's secret weapon and basketball's version of a cheat code. Picture this: he turns sideways, extends that endless arm to its full length, and flicks the ball in a high arc that kisses the sky before swishing through the net. Defenders might as well have been trying to block a shooting star. The skyhook was Lew's poetic ode to the game—a blend of physics, art, and a touch of "good luck stopping this!"

In his varsity debut, Lew orchestrated basketball. Averaging 29 points and 15.5 rebounds per game, he led the Bruins to an impeccable 30-0 season, snagging the NCAA championship like it was a foregone conclusion. He picked up the Most Outstanding Player award, probably running out of shelf space for all his trophies. The Bruins' dominance wasn't a one-hit wonder—they kept the hits coming with national titles in '68 and '69. Lew's personal accolades read like a grocery list: three-time First-Team All-American, two-time USBWA College Player of the Year—the man was a walking award ceremony.

But it wasn't all smooth sailing and slam dunks. In a move that felt as targeted as a tax audit, the NCAA introduced the "Alcindor Rule," banning dunking from 1967 to 1976—coincidence? We think not. Instead of throwing a tantrum, Lew simply pivoted, sharpening his skyhook until it was sharper than a chef's knife. On top of that, he navigated the choppy waters of racial tensions, bearing the weight of being a prominent African-American athlete during one of the most turbulent times in U.S. history. Challenges came at him from all angles, but Lew faced them head-on, as gracefully as he did opponents on the court.

Outside, Lew was flexing a different kind of muscle. He became deeply involved in social activism, standing shoulder to shoulder with icons of the era. In 1967, he attended the Cleveland Summit, where top black athletes convened to support Muhammad Ali's stand against the Vietnam War draft. A year later, he chose to boycott the Olympics, aligning with the Olympic Project for Human Rights in protest against racial injustice. These were symbolic gestures; and bold statements that echoed his unwavering commitment to civil rights and social justice. Lew was playing the game; but he was also changing it.

Meanwhile, in the classroom, Lew was no benchwarmer. Majoring in history, he dove deep into the annals of civilizations, connecting the dots between past and present like an academic Indiana Jones. Professors praised his insightful comments and his knack for linking historical events to modern-day issues. He was prepping for a career of skyhooks; and gearing up to be a well-informed, engaged citizen, ready to make a difference.

By the time he tossed his graduation cap, Lew had etched his name into the very fabric of NCAA basketball. First player ever to win the NCAA Tournament's Most Outstanding Player three times? Check. Leading UCLA to an eye-popping 88-2 record? Double-check. As he geared up to take on the professional ranks, he also embarked on a personal transformation. Inspired by his spiritual explorations, he converted to Islam, adopting the name Kareem Abdul-Jabbar, which translates to "noble servant of the Almighty." And there was a new name for a new chapter.

The 1969 NBA Draft had more buzz than a beehive. Kareem Abdul-Jabbar was the crown jewel every team wanted in their treasure chest. The Milwaukee Bucks and Phoenix Suns—both relatively new kids on the block—were neck and neck for the first pick. It all came down to a coin toss, the most nerve-wracking flip since man first spun a nickel. The coin favored the Bucks, and just like that, their franchise trajectory shot skyward faster than one of Kareem's skyhooks.

Stepping onto the court in a Bucks jersey, Kareem joined and supercharged the team. Averaging a staggering 28.8 points and 14.5 rebounds per game in his rookie season, he turned the Bucks from basement dwellers to playoff contenders with a dazzling 56-26 record. He snagged the NBA Rookie of the Year award—no surprise there—and became the main attraction wherever he played. Arenas filled up as fans clamored to see this basketball maestro perform his magic live.

The Bucks weren't done leveling up. In the 1970-71 season, they added Oscar Robertson to the mix—a veteran superstar who could do it all. It was like pairing fine wine with gourmet cheese; the combination was irresistible. Together, they propelled the Bucks to a league-best 66-16 record. Kareem picked up his first NBA MVP award, casually averaging 31.7 points and 16 rebounds per game. His skyhook remained the basketball equivalent of a magic trick—defenders watched helplessly as the ball sailed over their heads and into the net. On defense, he was a fortress, making even the bravest opponents think twice before venturing into the paint.

Come playoff time, the Bucks were a runaway train with no brakes. They swept the San Francisco Warriors, then took down the Los Angeles Lakers, punching their ticket to the NBA Finals against the Baltimore Bullets. Kareem cranked his performance up to eleven, averaging 27 points and 18.5 rebounds in the Finals. The Bucks did win—they swept the Bullets in four straight games, clinching the franchise's first NBA Championship. Kareem snagged the Finals MVP, cementing his status as one of the league's elite. It was official: Kareem Abdul-Jabbar was a superstar among superstars.

But off the hardwood, not everything was a slam dunk. Kareem faced racism and hostility, especially during road games where the crowd wasn't always friendly. In 1971, he publicly announced his conversion to Islam—a bold move that stirred up a whirlwind of reactions, not all of them positive. Critics and naysayers tried to rattle him, but Kareem stood firm, using his platform to foster cultural understanding and shatter stereotypes. He was defending the paint; and he was defending his principles.

In the seasons that followed, Kareem kept piling up accolades like they were going out of style. He snagged back-to-back MVP awards in 1972 and 1974, proving that excellence was his default setting. Despite his stellar play, the Bucks couldn't clinch another championship. Feeling the itch for a new challenge and a city that resonated with his cultural and personal vibes, Kareem requested a trade in 1974. He was ready for the next chapter, and the NBA was eager to see where he'd land.

In 1975, Kareem landed back in the City of Angels, traded to the Los Angeles Lakers. It was like returning to an old friend—the city where he'd once dominated the college scene. The Lakers, with their glittering legacy, were more than happy to welcome their new superstar. Kareem didn't disappoint. In his first season, he averaged a jaw-dropping 27.7 points, 16.9 rebounds, 5 assists, and 4.1 blocks per game. Oh, and he picked up another MVP award, because why not?

Kareem's time with the Lakers was about to get even more magical—literally. In 1979, the team drafted Earvin "Magic" Johnson, a point guard with enough charisma to power the Las Vegas Strip. Kareem's disciplined precision meshed perfectly with Magic's flashy exuberance. Together, they ignited the "Showtime" era, turning every game into a must-see spectacle. Fast breaks, no-look passes, skyhooks—the Lakers' games became the hottest ticket in town, and fans around the globe tuned in to catch the excitement.

The 1979-80 season was a basketball fairy tale come to life. Kareem nabbed his sixth MVP award—a record-setter—averaging 24.8 points, 10.8 rebounds, and 3.4 blocks per game. In the NBA Finals against the Philadelphia 76ers, he was a force of nature. But then, disaster struck: a severely sprained ankle in Game 5. With their captain sidelined, the Lakers could have crumbled. Instead, Magic Johnson, ever the showman, slid into the center position for Game 6. He delivered a legendary performance, leading the team to victory and securing the championship. Kareem's leadership and prior heroics were the backbone of their success, even when he wasn't on the court.

Through it all, the skyhook remained Kareem's trusty Excalibur—an unstoppable weapon that defenders couldn't crack. it was the embodiment of countless hours of practice, discipline, and a deep comprehension of basketball's finer points. Kareem didn't rely solely on talent; he was a pioneer in fitness, embracing yoga and martial arts to keep his body in peak condition. This holistic approach paid dividends, allowing him to perform at elite levels well into his career.

Off the court, Kareem was just as impactful. He penned articles and books, sharing his insights on social justice and history. Public speaking engagements and community programs became his avenues for promoting education and empowerment. His intellectual curiosity and courage to tackle tough issues set him apart, making him not just a basketball legend but a thought leader and role model.

Kareem Abdul-Jabbar's early pro years were about redefining the very essence of a professional athlete. He melded unmatched skill with a deep commitment to personal growth and making a positive impact on society. From that towering kid in Harlem to an NBA legend, his story is a masterclass in how talent, when paired with hard work, integrity, and relentless pursuit of excellence, can inspire generations to come.

Magic Johnson

THE ASCENT OF A COURT MAGICIAN

Okay, hoop dreamers and basketball aficionados! We're kicking things off with the incredible tale of Earvin "Magic" Johnson, the man who brought more magic to the court than a wizard with a tricked-out broomstick. Lansing, Michigan, 1959, that's when the universe decided to sprinkle some extra sparkle onto our planet and delivered a baby boy named Earvin Johnson Jr. to the proud parents, Christine and Earvin Sr.

If you think Magic got his name from birth, hold your horses, folks! Earvin was simply Earvin for quite a bit. He grew up in a bustling household with nine siblings, making his family's home feel like a constant party, but with less cake and more chores. His dad worked in a General Motors plant and did some trash collecting on the side – talk about work ethic! Christine, his mom, was a school custodian, a job that probably came with the side perk of extra-large stacks of homework for her kids.

Magic's first brush with basketball came from watching his dad play in pick-up games. His father had some serious moves, but young Earvin was enchanted. He fell in love with the sport faster than you can say "alley-oop." He'd dribble his basketball to school every morning, no matter the weather. Snowstorm? Rain? Heatwave? Didn't matter. That ball was practically glued to his hand. By the time Earvin hit high school, he was already turning heads. Attending Everett High School, he dominated the court like a colossus among mere mortals. That kid was so good at basketball that opposing teams would tremble in their sneakers at the sight of him. And then came the game that changed everything – the moment the nickname "Magic" was born.

It was a night like no other. Earvin dropped 36 points, snagged 18 rebounds, and dished out 16 assists in a single game. Fred Stabley Jr., a local sportswriter, watched in sheer awe. After witnessing this sorcery on the hardwood, Stabley dubbed him "Magic," and the name stuck like glue on a trophy. Magic has talent, but he also had this infectious smile that could light up a dimly lit gym. He had a knack for making everyone around him better, and his enthusiasm for the game was so contagious you'd need a face mask to avoid catching it. Under his leadership, Everett High School went on an epic run, winning the state championship during his senior year. It was like watching a superhero in action, and his powers were a sight to behold.

One of the things that set Magic apart was his ability to see the court like he had a pair of eyes on the back of his head. No-look passes, behind-the-back assists, and dazzling dribbles were all part of his daily routine. He could predict plays before they happened, like some kind of basketball Nostradamus. His high school games started drawing crowds not just from his school but from rival schools, neighboring towns, and anyone who had heard whispers of the teenage phenom with the magical touch. Now, if you think he was all basketball, you're wrong. Magic was a bona fide charmer off the court too. He was elected senior class president, which means he had the skills to both lead a team to victory and run a high school student council meeting without breaking a sweat. His charisma was so strong, it's a wonder he didn't get elected mayor of Lansing while he was at it.

But let's not forget the family that grounded him. His parents Earvin Sr. and Christine kept Magic humble, reminding him that no matter how many points he scored, he'd still have to take out the trash and mow the lawn. Those early lessons in hard work and humility stuck with him, shaping him into the player – and person – he'd become. So, as Magic Johnson left high school, he carried with him the hopes of an entire city. He was off to college, ready to sprinkle his fairy dust on a bigger stage. The best is yet to come!

Young Earvin Johnson, now known as Magic, fresh off a high school state championship, was about to take his talents to the next level. He wasn't heading far from home, choosing to stay in Michigan, but this time it was East Lansing that would be his new playground. Magic enrolled at Michigan State University, ready to dazzle the collegiate basketball world with his supernatural skills. If high school basketball seemed like Magic's personal show, college basketball was about to become a blockbuster hit with Magic as the leading star. The Spartans, under Coach Jud Heathcote, had snagged the ultimate recruit. The moment Magic stepped onto the court for Michigan State, the energy was electric. The campus buzzed with excitement, and the local sports bars probably had to double their popcorn orders.

From the get-go, Magic lived up to the hype. Standing at 6'9", he was a giant among point guards, and his versatility was jaw-dropping. One moment he was directing traffic on the court, and the next, he'd pull a rebound from the heavens, dash coast-to-coast, and dish a no-look pass that left defenders scratching their heads in bewilderment. His freshman season was a whirlwind, with Magic leading the Spartans to a Big Ten Conference title. But this was merely the prelude to the real magic show. Entering his sophomore year, Magic and his Spartans had their eyes set on the NCAA tournament. It wasn't going to be an easy journey, but with Magic steering the ship, anything seemed possible. The NCAA tournament in 1979 is one for the history books. Magic's biggest test came in the championship game against Indiana State, led by another future NBA legend, Larry Bird. This it was THE game. Over 35 million viewers tuned in, making it the most-watched college basketball game ever.

The tension was palpable. On one side, you had Larry Bird, the blond bomber from French Lick, Indiana, with his sharpshooting skills and scrappy playstyle. On the other, you had Magic, with his flash and flair, ready to orchestrate his team like a maestro conducting a symphony. From the tip-off, it was clear this was no ordinary clash. Every pass, every dribble, every shot was charged with the kind of electricity that could power a small city. Magic was unstoppable. He led the Spartans with precision, weaving through defenses, dropping dimes like a gumball machine, and scoring with effortless grace. The synergy between him and his teammates was otherworldly. The Spartans triumphed, and Magic was named the tournament's Most Outstanding Player. That game didn't just end with a championship trophy; it marked the beginning of one of the greatest rivalries in sports history, Magic vs. Bird. It was a rivalry that would later transcend college basketball and light up the NBA.

With the NCAA title under his belt, Magic's college career was like a dream. But dreams have a funny way of evolving, and for Magic, the next logical step was the NBA. The 1979 NBA Draft was on the horizon, and teams were salivating at the prospect of landing this basketball prodigy. The Los Angeles Lakers, thanks to a fortuitous coin toss win, had the first pick, and they knew exactly who they wanted. Imagine the scene: a young Magic Johnson, brimming with talent and charisma, standing on the precipice of the professional basketball world. The Lakers called his name, and just like that, Magic was headed to the glitz and glamour of Hollywood. The bright lights of Los Angeles were about to get a whole lot brighter.

Magic's journey from a Lansing kid dribbling a basketball to a college champion on the brink of NBA stardom was nothing short of extraordinary. He'd brought joy and excitement to Michigan State, and now he was ready to enchant the entire basketball universe. The next chapter in Magic's life was about to begin, and it promised to be a rollercoaster of epic proportions.

There we were: Magic Johnson, freshly minted college champion and ready to step onto the grand stage of the NBA. Los Angeles was calling, and the Lakers were poised to enter a new era of basketball brilliance. The year was 1979, and the Lakers had the golden ticket, the first overall pick in the NBA Draft, and they chose Magic. It was like pairing peanut butter with jelly or a cape with a superhero costume – a match made in basketball heaven.

Magic landed in LA with a grin that could power a solar farm and charisma that made Hollywood stars look like background extras. The Lakers already had some serious talent, including the legendary Kareem Abdul-Jabbar, who stood like a towering skyscraper with his skyhook that defied physics. Adding Magic to the mix was akin to adding rocket fuel to a bonfire. Magic's rookie season was nothing short of, well, magical. From the moment he stepped on the court, he brought an energy that turned every game into a spectacle. His playing style was revolutionary – here was a 6'9" point guard who could pass like a magician, score with finesse, and rebound like he had pogo sticks for legs. Lakers' games were suddenly the hottest ticket in town, with celebrities packing the Forum to watch the Magic show.

The highlight of Magic's rookie season came in the 1980 NBA Finals. The Lakers were up against the Philadelphia 76ers, and with the series tied 2-2, Game 5 took a dramatic turn when Kareem injured his ankle. It looked like a disaster for the Lakers, but Magic, in true heroic fashion, stepped up to the challenge. For Game 6, he started at center, a position he'd never played professionally, and delivered a performance for the ages. He scored 42 points, grabbed 15 rebounds, and dished out 7 assists, leading the Lakers to victory and clinching the championship. At just 20 years old, Magic was named Finals MVP, cementing his status as a basketball prodigy.

The Lakers of the 1980s, often referred to as the "Showtime Lakers," were a basketball juggernaut, and Magic was their conductor. The fast-break offense, high-flying dunks, and no-look passes were their signature, transforming basketball into a form of entertainment that rivaled the biggest Hollywood blockbusters. The Forum became the epicenter of excitement, where every game was a must-see event. Magic's rivalry with Larry Bird, which began in college, continued to flourish in the NBA. The Lakers and the Boston Celtics clashed repeatedly in epic battles that defined an era. Their matchups in the Finals were like titanic duels between two gladiators, each game a drama of its own. Magic vs. Bird went beyond basketball; it was a cultural phenomenon that captivated fans across the globe. These two legends pushed each other to new heights, and the NBA thrived because of it.

But Magic was more than a showman. He was a leader, a player who made everyone around him better. His court vision was unparalleled, his passing was like poetry in motion, and his ability to control the game's tempo was masterful. Teammates knew that if they were open, Magic would find them, often with a pass that seemed to defy logic and physics. His unselfish play and infectious enthusiasm galvanized the team and created a sense of camaraderie that was the hallmark of the Showtime Lakers.

Throughout the 1980s, Magic led the Lakers to five NBA championships (1980, 1982, 1985, 1987, and 1988), earning three Finals MVP awards in the process. His battles with the Celtics, particularly the duels with Bird, were legendary, and each championship run added to his growing legacy. The Lakers were the kings of the court, and Magic was their charismatic ruler. Magic's accolades piled up faster than a kid collecting trading cards. He was a 12-time NBA All-Star, a three-time league MVP, and a perennial All-NBA First Team selection. His smile, charm, and electric style of play made him one of the most beloved figures in sports. Magic's impact wasn't confined to the court; he became a global ambassador for the game, bringing joy and excitement to fans around the world.

But Magic's adventure had tough moments. Injuries and fierce competition tested his resolve, though his spirit remained unbreakable. He was a player who thrived under pressure, and his clutch performances became the stuff of legend. Whether it was a last-second shot or a critical pass in a tight game, Magic had an uncanny ability to deliver when it mattered most.

As the 1980s came to a close, Magic's influence on the game was undeniable. He had redefined the point guard position, transformed the Lakers into a dynasty, and created memories that would last a lifetime for fans. His career was a symphony of skill, leadership, and sheer joy for the game of basketball. The rise of Magic Johnson, from a kid with a dream in Lansing to a global icon and basketball legend. His story is one of talent, perseverance, and the sheer magic of believing in yourself. But remember, this isn't the end. Magic's legacy continues to inspire new generations, and his contributions to the game and beyond are a testament to his extraordinary journey.

Larry Bird

THE HICK FROM FRENCH LICK

Let me take you to a little town called West Baden Springs, Indiana, a place so small it makes your average garden gnome look like a giant. Now, the year is 1956, and in this sleepy town, a baby named Larry Bird came squawking into the world like a rooster that drank too much coffee. He was born to Georgia and Claude Bird on December 7th, and trust me, that date would eventually go down in basketball history as the day hoops got their next big thing.

Larry's family was a far cry from being rich. Larry had so little pocket money, he couldn't even pay attention! (Joking.) They lived in a modest house, the kind where you could see what your neighbors were having for dinner if you squinted hard enough through the walls. The Birds were a tight-knit family, and Larry had five siblings, making the household as lively as a three-ring circus on Saturday night.

Well, growing up in West Baden Springs wasn't like living in a theme park. There were no roller coasters or cotton candy stands—just a lot of open fields, some cows, and the occasional tractor parade. The town itself was split into two parts: West Baden and French Lick. Larry often crossed over to French Lick, a place known more for its mineral springs than for producing basketball prodigies. French Lick and West Baden were close enough that the locals joked you could throw a rock from one end and hit a chicken in the other. And yes, Larry tried it more than once.

Larry's early years were marked by simplicity. He attended Springs Valley High School, where he discovered that he could shoot a basketball better than most folks could shoot a slingshot. But before his hoop dreams took flight, his daily life involved chores, school, and trying to stay out of trouble, which in a small town often meant not stepping in something unpleasant while walking down the street. Larry's dad, Claude, worked construction and took any odd job he could find, while his mom, Georgia, was the backbone of the family, keeping everything from falling apart at the seams. Larry spent much of his childhood outdoors, playing games with his brothers and developing an uncanny ability to throw things accurately, whether it was a ball, a rock, or a snowball aimed right at his brother's head.

Even as a kid, Larry showed signs of the competitiveness that would later define his basketball career. He hated to lose at anything, whether it was marbles, checkers, or seeing who could spit a watermelon seed the farthest. Legend has it that one summer, Larry practiced spitting watermelon seeds so much he could hit a tin can from twenty feet away. Can you guess what that dedication would look like when he picked up a basketball!

One of the most significant aspects of Larry's childhood was his height. By the time he reached middle school, Larry had sprouted up like a weed in a cornfield. He was taller than most kids his age, which made him an asset in any sport involving a ball. But basketball, oh basketball, that was where Larry's heart lay, even before he fully realized it. In those days, basketball wasn't played on gleaming hardwood courts with cheering fans. No, sir. Larry's early games took place on cracked concrete courts with hoops that leaned more than the Tower of Pisa. The backboards were often pieces of plywood, and the nets, if they existed, were as tattered as an old scarecrow's hat. But none of that mattered to Larry. He played with a passion and intensity that made the dilapidated courts seem like Madison Square Garden.

Larry's family encouraged his love for the game, though they couldn't always provide the latest gear. His first basketball was a hand-me-down, and his shoes were often so worn out that you could see his toes peeking through. But Larry didn't care. He played barefoot if he had to, shooting hoops until the sun dipped below the horizon and then some. There were nights when Georgia had to drag him inside, warning him about catching a cold. Larry's response? "Cold can't guard me, Ma!"

It's said that Larry's shooting form, which would later become iconic, was honed during these countless hours of solitary practice. He developed an almost supernatural accuracy, hitting shot after shot from spots on the court that seemed impossible to the average person. He'd line up from the far end, squint his eyes, and let the ball fly, the swish of the net ringing out like a melody of success. The local kids knew Larry was something special, though they might not have guessed he'd one day be a basketball savant. They'd gather around to watch him play, trying to imitate his moves, but more often than not ending up flat on their backs or chasing the ball as it bounced away. Larry, ever the humble one, would laugh it off and give them pointers, his early coaching signs already showing.

Larry's childhood was filled with the kind of experiences that would shape his character: hard work, family values, and a relentless drive to be the best. Little did the folks of West Baden Springs and French Lick know, the lanky kid shooting hoops on the rundown courts would one day become a household name.

As Larry Bird transitioned into high school, the simplicity of his childhood began to intertwine with the emerging complexity of his basketball destiny. At Springs Valley High School, Larry quickly became the talk of the town. It wasn't because he grew taller than the corn stalks that dominated the Indiana landscape, but because he could make a basketball sing, dance, and practically perform magic tricks. Larry entered Springs Valley with a presence that commanded attention. His height, which by now exceeded six feet, combined with his gangly frame, made him look like a scarecrow brought to life. But what really got people talking was his undeniable talent on the court. Larry Bird had a way of turning the most mundane high school games into epic showdowns worthy of a national audience.

His high school career was characterized by jaw-dropping performances. Larry didn't simply play basketball; he orchestrated it. His passes were so precise they could thread a needle from across the gym. His shooting was so accurate that opponents often checked the ball for GPS haha. And his basketball IQ? Let's just say, if basketball had a version of Einstein, Larry Bird would have been the one writing the equations.

Springs Valley High School was soon the epicenter of basketball excitement. The gym was packed every game night, with fans squeezed together like sardines in a can, all eager to witness the Bird magic. Larry led his team to several victories, turning games into events where his every move was scrutinized and celebrated. His scoring records began to pile up faster than a squirrel collecting nuts for winter. By the time he graduated, Larry Bird had etched his name in the annals of high school basketball history, leaving behind a trail of defeated opponents and awestruck fans. Despite his high school success, Larry's journey was far from a straight path. He initially committed to play for coach Bob Knight at Indiana University, but the experience was overwhelming for the shy, small-town boy. The bustling campus and intense atmosphere of Indiana University were a stark contrast to the quiet life he knew. After less than a month, Larry packed his bags and returned to French Lick, a decision that left many wondering if his basketball career would end before it truly began.

Back in French Lick, Larry took a break from basketball, working various odd jobs, including a stint as a garbage collector. Larry Bird, the future basketball legend, was tossing trash bags instead of basketballs. But it was during this period of introspection that Larry's passion for the game reignited. Realizing that his talent was too great to waste, he decided to give college basketball another shot, this time at Indiana State University in Terre Haute. Indiana State University wasn't actually a powerhouse in college basketball, but Larry Bird was about to change that. From the moment he stepped on campus, it was clear that the Sycamores had acquired a game-changer. Larry's presence was like adding jet fuel to a lawnmower. His impact was immediate and profound, turning the team's fortunes around with the speed of a fast break.

The transformation Larry brought to Indiana State was ... hum ... miraculous. He led the Sycamores to an undefeated regular season and a berth in the NCAA tournament, something the school had never achieved before. The 1978-1979 season became legendary, with Larry Bird at the center of it all. His play was so captivating that it turned Indiana State games into must-see events, with fans and media flocking to witness his exploits. The climax of Larry's college career came in the 1979 NCAA Championship game, where Indiana State faced off against Michigan State, led by another future NBA star, Magic Johnson. The game was billed as a clash of titans, a David vs. Goliath story with both Davids and Goliaths on each side. The hype surrounding the game was immense, and it didn't disappoint. Larry and Magic went head-to-head in a battle that captured the imagination of basketball fans across the nation.

While Indiana State ultimately lost the game, Larry Bird's performance throughout the season and the championship clash cemented his status as one of the greatest college players of all time. He finished his college career with numerous accolades, including the Naismith College Player of the Year award. More importantly, he had put Indiana State on the basketball map and set the stage for what would come next. But before we get ahead of ourselves, let's pause to appreciate what Larry Bird achieved during his high school and college years. He transformed from a lanky, small-town kid into a basketball phenomenon, leaving an indelible mark on the sport at every level he played. His journey through high school heroics and college glory was filled with hard work, dedication, and an unrelenting drive to be the best. The legend of Larry Bird was well on its way...

With his college career behind him, Larry Bird stood on the precipice of a new chapter, one that would catapult him from local hero to global icon. The year was 1979, and the Boston Celtics, a franchise steeped in championship tradition, had secured the rights to draft Bird. The Celtics, desperate to return to their glory days, saw in Larry a potential savior. And Larry? Well, he saw a new arena for his talents, one that stretched far beyond the cracked courts of Indiana.

Bird's entry into the NBA was so good. He signed a then-record rookie contract, signaling to everyone that he meant business. The Boston Garden, with its creaky floors and raucous fans, became Larry's new stage. From his first game, it was clear that Bird was a different breed of player. He combined an old-school work ethic with an almost mystical understanding of the game. His debut season was a revelation, as he led the Celtics to a remarkable turnaround, improving their win total by 32 games from the previous year.

Larry's rookie year was a masterclass in basketball excellence. He averaged 21.3 points, 10.4 rebounds, and 4.5 assists per game, showcasing his all-around ability. His performances were a blend of artistry and grit, each game a canvas where he painted masterpieces with every dribble, pass, and shot. Larry's play earned him the NBA Rookie of the Year award, and he was selected to the All-Star team, a rare feat for a newcomer. You would think only the stats that made Larry Bird special. Not only that! It was his swagger, his unshakeable confidence, and his trash-talking prowess. Yes, Larry Bird was one of the greatest trash talkers the game has ever seen. Opponents would be on the receiving end of his verbal jabs, often left stunned by his audacity and precision. Bird had an uncanny ability to back up every word with action, making him a feared and respected competitor.

Bird's arrival also reignited the storied Celtics-Lakers rivalry. The 1980s became defined by epic showdowns between Larry Bird and Magic Johnson, the two players who had faced off in the 1979 NCAA Championship game. Their rivalry was the stuff of legend, a Shakespearean drama played out on the hardwood. Magic's Lakers were the flashy, high-flying "Showtime" squad, while Bird's Celtics were the blue-collar, no-nonsense team that embodied Boston's gritty spirit.

The 1981 NBA Finals marked the beginning of Bird's championship journey with the Celtics. Facing the Houston Rockets, Bird led Boston to its 14th NBA title. His clutch performances, leadership, and sheer will to win were on full display. Larry averaged 15.3 points, 15.3 rebounds, and 7 assists per game in the series, securing his first Finals MVP award. The victory was a testament to his ability to elevate those around him and to his unyielding desire for greatness. As the 1980s progressed, Bird continued to redefine what it meant to be an NBA superstar. His rivalry with Magic and the Lakers reached new heights in the 1984 NBA Finals, a series often cited as one of the greatest in history. The seven-game slugfest was a rollercoaster of emotions, with Bird and Magic trading blows like heavyweight fighters. Bird's heroics in Game 7, where he scored 20 points and grabbed 12 rebounds, led the Celtics to victory and earned him his second Finals MVP award.

Larry's brilliance on the court was matched by his dedication to his craft. He was the first to arrive at practice and the last to leave, always honing his skills, always striving for perfection. His shooting drills became the stuff of legend, with teammates and coaches marveling at his relentless pursuit of excellence. Bird's work ethic was infectious, inspiring his teammates to push their limits and embody the same dedication. The 1985-86 season is often considered Bird's magnum opus. He won his third consecutive MVP award, joining the ranks of only Bill Russell and Wilt Chamberlain. Bird averaged 25.8 points, 9.8 rebounds, and 6.8 assists per game that season, leading the Celtics to a 67-15 record. The team's depth and talent, combined with Bird's leadership, made them nearly unstoppable.

The 1986 NBA Finals saw the Celtics face the Houston Rockets once again. Bird's performance in the Finals was a tour de force. He averaged 24 points, 9.7 rebounds, and 9.5 assists per game, leading Boston to its 16th NBA championship. His crowning moment came in Game 6, where he notched a triple-double with 29 points, 11 rebounds, and 12 assists, earning his third Finals MVP award. Larry Bird had reached the pinnacle of basketball, cementing his legacy as one of the greatest to ever play the game.

Bird's early professional career was a blend of individual brilliance and team success. He transformed the Celtics, restored their championship pedigree, and gave the fans memories that would last a lifetime. His rivalry with Magic elevated the NBA to new heights, captivating audiences and turning basketball into a global phenomenon. As we close this chapter on Larry Bird's early professional years, Lest's remember his journey from a small-town kid in Indiana to an NBA legend was marked by hard work, resilience, and an unyielding passion for the game. Bird's story is one of triumph, a testament to what can be achieved with talent, dedication, and a little bit of that Bird magic.

Bill Russell

CHAMPION, INNOVATOR, ACTIVIST

Let's crank the time machine way back to 1934, to a place called Monroe, Louisiana. The year is 1934, where the world is still getting used to the whole idea of talking movies, and little William Felton Russell is born into a family that could barely afford a loaf of bread, let alone a basketball. The world has no idea yet, but it's just gained one of the greatest shot-blockers ever. Young Bill wasn't born with a silver spoon in his mouth. Heck, he probably didn't even have a plastic one. His early years were tough, and life in Monroe wasn't a Disney fairy tale. It was more like one of those classic black-and-white films where the hero emerges from rags to riches through grit and determination.

Now, let's fast forward a bit to Bill's childhood. We're talking about a young kid who spent his days running around in the dusty streets of West Monroe. It's hot, it's humid, and little Bill has already started to grow into those famously long legs. The Russells, like many African American families in the South during the 1930s and 1940s, faced their fair share of discrimination and hardship. But Bill's dad, Charlie, was a strong-willed man who wasn't about to let anything break his spirit. He taught Bill the value of hard work, integrity, and standing up for what's right. By the time Bill reached high school age, the family had moved to Oakland, California. The move was a game-changer. You see, the Bay Area offered more opportunities, although things were far from perfect. Bill attended McClymonds High School, where his basketball journey truly began. And let me tell you, if you think Bill was an instant star, think again. The guy got cut from the junior varsity team initially. Yep, the basketball legend himself didn't even make the team at first. But he had something a lot of people didn't – perseverance and a wingspan that probably made birds jealous.

Bill's high school coach, George Powles, saw potential in this lanky kid who could seemingly touch the moon when he jumped. Powles believed in Bill when few others did. With guidance and relentless practice, Bill transformed from a kid who could barely dribble to a defensive monster. His ability to block shots and grab rebounds was otherworldly. Opponents must have felt like they were trying to score against a human wall. After high school, Russell's skills earned him a scholarship to the University of San Francisco (USF). USF might not have had a strong basketball reputation at the time, but Bill and K.C. Jones changed that quickly, creating excitement with their plays. If you're picturing a dramatic sports movie montage right now, you're not far off. Bill's college years were legendary.

From 1953 to 1956, the USF Dons were the hottest ticket in town. Under the coaching of Phil Woolpert, Russell's defense-first mentality revolutionized the game. You have to understand, back then, basketball was all about scoring. Defense was an afterthought. But Bill Russell? He was swatting shots left and right, snagging rebounds like he had glue on his hands, and running the court with the grace of a gazelle. During his tenure at USF, the Dons won 55 consecutive games, an unprecedented streak that left opponents shaking their heads in disbelief. Bill was redefining Basketball. His team won back-to-back NCAA championships in 1955 and 1956, making them the first team to do so. In 1956, Bill also played a crucial role in leading the U.S. Olympic basketball team to a gold medal in Melbourne. The guy was a one-man wrecking crew. Russell's dominance at USF was a preview of the havoc he'd wreak in the professional league, but we're getting ahead of ourselves here. Back to college Bill – he was a beast on the court; he was also an advocate for civil rights, even at a young age. His time in San Francisco was about more than basketball; it was about growing into a leader, both in sports and society.

Bill's journey from a dusty Louisiana town to college basketball superstardom is the stuff legends are made of. And we haven't even scratched the surface of his professional career yet. That's up next, where the NBA world is about to get its socks knocked off by this defensive dynamo.

We're diving now into the thrilling saga of Bill Russell's entry into the NBA and how he shook the Boston Celtics like a storm in a snow globe. It's 1956, and the Boston Celtics, led by the cunning Red Auerbach, are scouting for that one game-changing piece. They're eyeing this 6'10" powerhouse from USF who's been causing a ruckus on every court he steps on. When the Celtics snagged Bill Russell in a draft day trade, it was like they had found the final piece of a basketball jigsaw puzzle that no one else even realized was missing. Russell joined a team that already had some notable talents, but they were missing that defensive anchor, that dominant force in the paint. And boy, did Russell fill that void. From day one, he hit the hardwood with the intensity of a thousand suns. In his rookie season, Russell averaged an eye-popping 19.6 rebounds per game. Nineteen-point-six! That's not a typo. It's almost like he had a magnetic force field drawing every loose ball his way.

Russell's defensive prowess were revolutionary as well. He made blocking shots look as easy as swatting flies, and his ability to alter the trajectory of a game with his sheer presence was unprecedented. He was a basketball alchemist, turning defensive plays into gold. And let's not forget his knack for starting fast breaks with his quick outlet passes. It's like he had eyes on the back of his head, always knowing where his teammates were. The Celtics weren't an immediate overnight success, but with Russell anchoring the defense, the team's fortunes turned around quickly. The 1956-57 season saw the Celtics capture their first NBA championship, with Russell leading the charge. That season, the Celtics' defense was like a brick wall, and Russell was the cornerstone. They defeated the St. Louis

Hawks in a nail-biting seven-game series, and the league started to realize that Bill Russell was no ordinary rookie.

Russell's unique blend of athleticism, intelligence, and sheer willpower changed the game. He wasn't all about scoring points; he knew that defense wins championships. His impact was so profound that he effectively invented the role of the defensive specialist in the NBA. Coaches began to understand the importance of having a player who could dominate on the defensive end, and teams around the league started to look for their own version of Bill Russell – not that they'd find one, of course. From 1957 onwards, the Celtics became a basketball dynasty. Red Auerbach's master plan revolved around Russell's defensive genius and unselfish play. The Celtics' fast-break offense, often ignited by Russell's rebounds and quick passes, was unstoppable. They played as a cohesive unit, with Russell setting the tone for teamwork and hustle. It wasn't rare to see him diving for loose balls, sprinting down the court, or making a crucial block that would send the crowd into a frenzy. Throughout the late 1950s and 1960s, the Celtics were a juggernaut, clinching championship after championship. Russell collected rings like they were going out of style, ending up with eleven NBA titles by the time he hung up his sneakers. And let's talk about those epic battles with Wilt Chamberlain. It was like watching two titans clash, each game a gladiatorial contest that left fans breathless. Russell and Chamberlain pushed each other to the limits, with Russell often getting the upper hand due to his tenacity and team-oriented play.

One of the most remarkable aspects of Russell's career was his leadership. In 1966, he became the player-coach of the Celtics, a role that was practically unheard of at the time. Leading a team while still being a dominant force on the court? That's like being the captain of a ship while also navigating through a storm. Yet Russell did it with grace and success, leading the Celtics to two more championships as a player-coach. His calm demeanor and strategic mind made him an excellent coach, and his teammates respected him immensely. Russell's impact wasn't confined to the hardwood. Off the court, he was a fierce advocate for civil rights and equality. During a time when America was grappling with significant social upheaval, Russell stood tall, using his platform to speak out against injustice and racism. His courage and integrity extended far beyond basketball, making him a pivotal figure in the broader struggle for human rights.

By the time 1969 rolled around, Russell had cemented his place as a basketball legend. His career was a testament to the power of defense, teamwork, and sheer determination.

The Boston Celtics' era of dominance was largely built on the foundation that Russell laid down, and his influence on the game of basketball was immeasurable. From a kid who couldn't make his high school JV team to a player who transformed the NBA, Bill Russell's journey is the stuff of legends.

As we venture into Bill Russell's extraordinary career with the Boston Celtics, we find ourselves smack dab in the 1960s, a decade bursting with change, challenges, and triumphant basketball. By now, Russell had firmly established himself as the cornerstone of the Celtics' dynasty, a towering figure both on and off the court.

Let's kick things off in the early 60s, a time when the Celtics were dominating the NBA like a pack of hungry wolves in a league full of sheep. The 1960-61 season was a classic example. The Celtics, with Russell anchoring the defense, racked up an impressive record and bulldozed their way through the playoffs. The Finals saw them face off against the St. Louis Hawks again, and Russell's defense was really good. He was like a one-man barricade, blocking shots, snagging rebounds, and frustrating opponents to no end. The Celtics clinched the championship, and Russell added another shiny ring to his growing collection. But life wasn't all smooth sailing and slam dunks. The mid-60s brought about some of the most intense rivalries in NBA history. One name that looms large during this period is Wilt Chamberlain. Wilt was a behemoth, a scoring machine, and a constant thorn in Russell's side. The battles between these two giants were the stuff of legends. Every game was a clash of titans, with Russell's defensive prowess pitted against Chamberlain's scoring juggernaut. Yet, time and again, Russell's Celtics found ways to emerge victorious, proving that teamwork and defense often trump individual brilliance.

Now, let's not forget the 1965 Eastern Conference Finals against the Philadelphia 76ers, a series that delivered one of the most iconic moments in NBA history. Picture this: Game 7, the Celtics clinging to a slim lead in the final seconds, and the 76ers' Hal Greer attempting to inbound the ball. Russell, with his instincts as sharp as a hawk, deflects the pass, leading to the famous Johnny Most call, "Havlicek stole the ball!" This clutch defensive play sealed the victory and sent the Celtics to another NBA Finals, where they would once again come out on top. As the 60s rolled on, the Celtics faced not only fierce competition on the court but also the evolving social landscape off it. Russell, never one to shy away from the issues of his time, found himself at the forefront of the civil rights movement. In a period marked by significant social upheaval, Russell's activism and outspokenness added another layer to his already impressive legacy. He wasn't merely a basketball player; he was a voice for change, standing up against racism and injustice, even when it meant facing hostility and prejudice.

The 1966 season brought a new challenge: Russell became the first African American head coach in NBA history, while still playing for the Celtics. Talk about wearing two hats! The transition wasn't easy, but if anyone was up to the task, it was Bill Russell. His leadership was unparalleled, both as a player and a coach. He guided the Celtics to yet another championship, proving that his strategic mind was as sharp as his defensive skills. By the late 60s, the Celtics were an aging team, and the competition was getting stiffer. Yet, Russell's indomitable spirit kept them in the hunt for titles. The 1968-69 season was particularly dramatic. The Celtics, perceived as underdogs, clawed their way through the playoffs, defying the odds at every turn. The Finals saw them face the formidable Los Angeles Lakers, led by Wilt Chamberlain, Jerry West, and Elgin Baylor. It was a showdown for the ages, a battle that would go down in history. The series stretched to a decisive Game 7, played in the hostile environment of the Lakers' home court. The pressure was immense, but Russell, with his characteristic calm and determination, rallied his team. In a nail-biting finish, the Celtics emerged victorious, securing their 11th championship in Russell's 13-year career. It was a fitting end to an era, a testament to Russell's greatness and his ability to inspire those around him.

Reflecting on Russell's career, it's impossible not to marvel at the sheer breadth of his achievements. Eleven NBA championships, five MVP awards, and countless records that stand to this day. Yet, perhaps his most significant contribution was his unwavering commitment to excellence, equality, and leadership. He showed the world that basketball was more than a game; it was a platform for change, a stage for showcasing not just physical prowess but also moral courage. Bill Russell's career with the Boston Celtics was a masterclass in resilience, determination, and innovation. His impact on the game of basketball is immeasurable, a legacy built on sweat, strategy, and an unyielding spirit.

Wilt Chamberlain

THE TOWERING LEGACY

So, let's zoom back to August 21, 1936, to a city called Philadelphia. Why, you ask? Because on this very day, a baby who would grow up to be one of the tallest, most dominating basketball players of all time, was born. His name? Wilton Norman Chamberlain. But let's call him Wilt, because that's what his friends called him, and after all, we're all friends here, right? Baby Wilt probably didn't even know what basketball was at that point. He was busy doing baby things like eating, sleeping, and growing. Oh boy, did he grow. While other kids were barely adding an inch or two each year, Wilt seemed to be in a hurry to touch the sky. By the time he was ten, he was already six feet tall. That's like being taller than your average fifth-grade teacher while you're still trying to figure out fractions.

Growing up in the 1940s and early 1950s in Philadelphia, Wilt's height made him stand out like a giraffe among goats. Naturally, this made him a bit self-conscious. But let's be real, being tall isn't exactly the worst thing that can happen to you, especially when you're about to become a basketball legend. While other kids were collecting baseball cards or mastering the art of hula hooping, Wilt was being introduced to a game that would change his life forever: basketball. Wilt attended Overbrook High School, and it didn't take long for people to realize that he wasn't just tall—he was also incredibly athletic. His high school coach, Cecil Mosenson, probably thought he hit the jackpot. It's like finding out your goldfish is really a magical sea serpent. Wilt could run fast, jump high, and had this uncanny ability to score baskets like they were going out of style. It was here that Wilt started to show the world a glimpse of his future greatness.

At Overbrook, Wilt was a scoring machine. In one game, he scored 90 points. Yes, you read that right, 90 points! That's more points than most entire teams score in a game. The defender tasked with guarding him has no chance, like trying to stop a runaway freight train with a butterfly net. And the crowd? They might need scoreboards with extra digits to keep up with Wilt's antics on the court. Wilt had many interests beyond basketball, though. He tried his hand at track and field, too. High jump, long jump, running races—you name it, he did it. If there was a sport that required jumping over or running past something, Wilt was your guy. It's like he was on a mission to break every athletic record at Overbrook High School, and spoiler alert: he pretty much did. But let's not get ahead of ourselves. There are moments when young Wilt takes a break from the court or the track. Like any other kid, he had to deal with homework, chores, and, of course, the occasional sibling rivalry. Wilt had eight siblings, so you can bet there were some epic battles for the last cookie or the best seat in front of the radio.

Despite his towering presence and undeniable talent, Wilt had to work on his skills. He didn't wake up one day and dunk over everyone like a superhero. He practiced hard, learned from his mistakes, and kept improving. He had this incredible drive to be the best, which meant hours of practice, even when he could have been out having fun. His friends probably called him crazy, but in hindsight, it's clear Wilt had his eyes on a much bigger prize. Being a teenager in the 1950s and dunking in games when most players could barely touch the rim must have been incredible. Wilt made the crowd go wild. People came from all over to see this high school phenom who played like he had springs in his shoes. He was the talk of the town, and soon, the entire country was buzzing about this basketball prodigy from Philadelphia.

By the time Wilt finished high school, he had already set countless records, won numerous awards, and established himself as a force to be reckoned with. College scouts from all over the nation were practically camping outside his house, hoping to convince him to join their team. It's like when your favorite band announces a surprise concert, and everyone scrambles to get tickets. Wilt was the hottest ticket in town. His high school period was simply remarkable. He grew from a tall, self-conscious kid into a basketball superstar with skills and charisma that left fans and opponents alike in awe. As he prepared to leave Overbrook and take his talents to the college level, the world of basketball could hardly wait to see what this giant of a teenager would do next.

As Wilt Chamberlain wrapped up his illustrious high school career, his journey was not over. The world of college basketball was eagerly awaiting his arrival, and the University of Kansas was the lucky school to land him. There was Wilt, a young man bursting with talent and ambition, arriving in Lawrence, Kansas, a place that probably didn't know what hit it.

The decision to attend Kansas wasn't out of the blue. Wilt was swayed by the legendary coach Phog Allen, a man who was practically a basketball wizard himself. Allen convinced Wilt that Kansas was the place where he could refine his skills and prepare for the professional stage. So, in 1955, Wilt packed his bags and headed to the heartland of America, ready to leave an indelible mark on college basketball. Wilt's freshman year at Kansas was a bit of a waiting game. Freshmen can now play varsity sports. The excitement is palpable! Wilt, the basketball prodigy, is finally on the court with the varsity team. But he didn't waste his time moping around. Instead, he played for the freshman team, and boy, did he dominate. His presence on the court was like a lion playing with a bunch of house cats. Spectators came in droves to watch him, even if it was just a freshman game. It was clear that something monumental was brewing.

By his sophomore year, Wilt was fully active in the varsity scene, delivering impressive performances. In his very first varsity game, he scored 52 points and grabbed 31 rebounds. Yes, you heard that right. Those are numbers that would make even the greatest players of all time do a double-take. Wilt was a force of nature, and he played the game with a blend of power and grace that had never been seen before. Playing for the Kansas Jayhawks, Wilt led the team to an impressive season. His skills on the court were jaw-dropping: towering over opponents, swatting shots away like annoying flies, and scoring at will. It was as if he had his own personal trampoline hidden in his shoes, allowing him to soar above everyone else. The fans were in love, the opponents were terrified, and the college basketball world was buzzing with Wiltmania.

One of the most memorable moments of Wilt's college career came during the 1957 NCAA championship game against the University of North Carolina. It was a battle for the ages, with Wilt leading the Jayhawks against a well-oiled Tar Heels team. The game went into triple overtime, and although Kansas lost by a single point, Wilt's performance was legendary. He scored 23 points and grabbed 14 rebounds despite being double- and triple-teamed the entire game. It was a heartbreaking loss, but it cemented Wilt's status as a college basketball icon. Wilt's college days were a storm of intense passions, with basketball just a single flash of lightning. He brings an unforgettable charisma and sense of humor to the campus scene. He participated in various activities and even tried his hand at acting in school plays. His classmates were often in awe of his talents both on and off the court. Wilt stands as both an athlete and a marvel. Despite his success, Wilt faced significant challenges during his college years. Being an African American athlete in the 1950s came with its own set of obstacles. He encountered racial prejudice and discrimination, both on and off the court. But Wilt's resilience and determination were unwavering. He used these experiences to fuel his desire to be the best, to break barriers, and to pave the way for future generations of athletes.

As Wilt's time at Kansas came to an end, the next chapter of his life was eagerly anticipated by everyone who had witnessed his dominance. He had achieved everything possible in college basketball, but the professional stage beckoned. The NBA was about to get its first taste of Wilt Chamberlain, and the league would never be the same again. Wilt Chamberlain's college career was a whirlwind of spectacular performances and unforgettable moments. He left an indelible mark on the University of Kansas, setting records and thrilling fans. His legacy as one of the greatest college basketball players of all time was secure, and his journey was far from over. The professional stage awaited, and Wilt was ready to take his game to new heights.

⬤

So there Wilt stood, at the threshold of the NBA, ready to shake the very foundations of professional basketball. When the 1959 NBA Draft rolled around, the Philadelphia Warriors had the first pick, and they snapped up Wilt faster than you can say "slam dunk." Wilt, at an impressive 7 feet 1 inch, is stepping into the league ready to make history. In Wilt's rookie season, he averaged 37.6 points and 27 rebounds per game. These aren't typographical errors; these are actual stats that would make any player's career look like child's play. And this was just his rookie season. The basketball world had seen tall players before, but never someone with Wilt's combination of size, athleticism, and skill. Defenders were left scratching their heads, trying to figure out how to stop this human skyscraper from scoring at will.

Wilt's rivalry with Bill Russell of the Boston Celtics is the stuff of legend. Imagine two titans clashing every time their teams met. Bill Russell was known for his defensive prowess and team-oriented play, while Wilt was the unstoppable scoring machine. Their battles were epic, filled with high drama, intense competition, and mutual respect. While Russell's Celtics often got the better of Wilt's teams in terms of championships, Wilt was never overshadowed. He continued to put up mind-boggling numbers, setting records that still stand today. In the 1961-62 season, Wilt did something that might as well be straight out of a comic book. On March 2, 1962, in a game against the New York Knicks, Wilt scored 100 points. One hundred points in a single game! That's like a baseball player hitting ten home runs in one game. The arena in Hershey, Pennsylvania, was filled with fans who could hardly believe what they were witnessing. Wilt was so dominant that the Knicks' defenders probably needed counseling after that game. This legendary feat remains one of the most iconic moments in sports history. But Wilt wasn't content with being a scorer. He wanted to be the best all-around player, which meant improving his passing, defense, and teamwork. In the 1966-67 season, playing for the Philadelphia 76ers, Wilt led his team to an NBA championship. That season, he showcased his versatility by leading the league in assists, proving that he could do more than score. He was a complete player, a leader, and a champion.

Wilt Chamberlain's career is filled with statistical anomalies that boggle the mind. He scored 50 or more points in a game 118 times. He once averaged 50.4 points per game over an entire season. He never fouled out of a game in his entire career, which is astonishing given his physical style of play. His rebounding prowess was unmatched, pulling down 55 rebounds in a single game against the Celtics in 1960. These records make you wonder if Wilt was even human or some kind of basketball supercomputer sent from the future. Off the court, Wilt brings a tremendous presence. He had a personality as big as his stature, often entertaining fans and teammates with his humor and charisma. He loved to challenge himself in different sports, from volleyball to track and field, proving that his athletic talents were not confined to the basketball court. Wilt's confidence was legendary, and he often spoke about his achievements with a mix of pride and humor.

Wilt's career had its fair share of intriguing stories. His unmatched talent often led to criticism from detractors who argued that he should have won more championships given his individual brilliance. But Wilt didn't let the critics get to him. He knew his worth and continued to play the game with the same passion and determination that had driven him since his high school days. One of the most interesting chapters in Wilt's career came when he joined the Los Angeles Lakers in 1968. Teaming up with legends like Jerry West and Elgin Baylor, Wilt continued to dominate the court. In 1972, he helped the Lakers win an NBA championship, solidifying his legacy as a winner and a game-changer. That season, the Lakers also set a record with a 33-game winning streak, a record that still stands. Wilt played a crucial role in that streak, anchoring the defense and contributing on offense.

Wilt Chamberlain's NBA career was a rollercoaster of incredible highs and a few frustrating lows. But through it all, he remained one of the most compelling and influential figures in the sport. His impact on the game was profound, as he forced the NBA to change rules to accommodate his dominant style of play. For instance, they widened the lane to prevent him from scoring so easily and changed goaltending rules because of his defensive capabilities. When Wilt finally hung up his sneakers in 1973, he left behind a legacy that would inspire generations of players. His career averages of 30.1 points and 22.9 rebounds per game are mind-boggling, and his influence on the game is immeasurable. Wilt Chamberlain was an icon, a trailblazer, and a legend whose story will be told for generations to come.

Tim Duncan

A JOURNEY FROM SWIMMER TO NBA ICON

Tim Duncan's story starts in a place you might not expect for a future basketball legend—the beautiful, sun-kissed island of Saint Croix in the U.S. Virgin Islands. A young Timmy is running around barefoot on sandy beaches, his gangly legs kicking up the salty air. Little did anyone know, this island kid would grow up to become one of the greatest basketball players in history. But before the hoop dreams, Tim had different aquatic aspirations.

Born on April 25, 1976, Timothy Theodore Duncan (yeah, that middle name is a mouthful) initially dreamed of making waves, quite literally, as an Olympic swimmer. His older sister, Tricia, was already making a splash in swimming, and Tim wanted to follow in her wake. He trained diligently in the pool, his long limbs slicing through the water with the grace of a dolphin. But life, as we all know, has a funny way of flipping the script. When Hurricane Hugo hit Saint Croix in 1989, it devastated the island, including the only Olympic-sized swimming pool. Tim's swimming dreams seemed to sink with the storm. With the pool out of commission, Tim found himself at a crossroads. What do you do when your dream is washed away by a hurricane? Well, if you're Tim Duncan, you pivot. Literally. He took his talents to the basketball court, and oh boy, what a pivot that turned out to be.

Now, let's pause for a second. Tim Duncan, a 13-year-old Tim Duncan, all 6 feet of him, was dribbling a basketball for the first time. He was awkward, uncoordinated, and, let's be frank, probably tripping over his own feet half the time. But here's where the story gets interesting. Tim's height was already making him stand out like a palm tree in a potato patch. His natural athleticism, honed by years in the pool, translated surprisingly well to basketball. Plus, he had one thing that many kids his age lacked: perseverance. Enter Al Keith, a local legend and basketball coach who saw potential in the lanky teenager. Coach Keith took Tim under his wing, teaching him the fundamentals of the game. He drilled into Tim the importance of footwork, positioning, and, most importantly, patience. If you've ever seen Tim Duncan play, you know that patience became his trademark. On the court, he moved with the calm precision of a chess grandmaster, always a step ahead of his opponents. Tim's improvement was rapid. He grew more confident with each game, his movements becoming more fluid, his shots more accurate. By the time he reached high school at St. Dunstan's Episcopal, he was already a force to be reckoned with. His height soared to 6'8", and he dominated the local basketball scene, leading his team to multiple victories. But despite his growing prowess, Tim remained humble and grounded, a gentle giant who preferred to let his game do the talking.

Word of the island prodigy spread, and soon enough, college scouts were making the trip to Saint Croix to see him in action. One scout, Dave Odom from Wake Forest University, saw something truly special in Tim. Odom was so impressed that he offered Tim a scholarship on the spot. Tim, ever the cautious and thoughtful individual, weighed his options carefully. Ultimately, he decided to take a leap of faith and head to the mainland

United States, a place as foreign to him as the idea of snow in the Caribbean. And so, in 1993, Tim Duncan found himself in Winston-Salem, North Carolina, at Wake Forest University. It was a new chapter, filled with challenges and opportunities that would shape him into the legend we know today.

So, here we are. Tim Duncan, the island boy with a swimmer's dream, landed in the bustling world of American college basketball at Wake Forest University. Tim stood out on campus with his 6'10" frame, likely searching for familiar palm trees. But more than the climate, it was the culture and the game of basketball itself that was about to undergo a transformation. From day one, Tim stood out as a unique college freshman. His quiet demeanor and intense focus set him apart. Coach Dave Odom quickly realized that this young man wasn't there to mess around. He was there to learn, grow, and most importantly, win. However, Tim's first year was not all slam dunks and highlight reels. He played sparingly as a freshman, averaging a modest 9.8 points and 9.6 rebounds per game. It was a year of adjustment, learning the ropes of the college game, and adapting to the fast-paced style of play.

Wake Forest hadn't seen a player like Tim in years. His skill set was unique: he combined the agility and grace of a swimmer with the burgeoning power of a basketball player still growing into his frame. By his sophomore year, Tim had made his mark. His stats surged to 16.8 points, 12.5 rebounds, and 3.98 blocks per game, earning him the title of ACC Defensive Player of the Year. Tim's shot-blocking ability was otherworldly; opponents found themselves regularly thwarted by his impeccably timed jumps and relentless defense. It was like trying to score against a moving brick wall.

Tim's college career included many colorful characters. His Wake Forest teammates quickly learned that Tim was the ultimate prankster. Tim often sneaks into the dorms to place alarm clocks under his teammates' beds, all set to go off at random times during the night. Or the time he filled Coach Odom's office with hundreds of balloons, leaving the coach to pop his way to his desk. Tim's humor was as dry as it was sharp, and his antics kept the team's spirits high even during the toughest of seasons. By his junior year, Tim Duncan had become a national sensation. He was the rock around which the team was built. His stats were jaw-dropping: 19.1 points, 12.3 rebounds, and 3.76 blocks per game. He led Wake Forest to back-to-back ACC championships, a feat that hadn't been achieved in over 30 years. The Demon Deacons were a force to be reckoned with, and Tim Duncan was the undisputed leader, even if he preferred to let his actions speak louder than his words .

Off the court, Tim was majoring in psychology. Yes, the Big Fundamental was also the Big Brainiac. He found the subject fascinating, particularly how the human mind works under pressure. His interest in psychology adds to his calm, composed demeanor on the court. While other players might crack under the weight of expectations, Tim remained unflappable, a cool customer in the heat of battle. One of the most memorable moments of Tim's college career came during his senior year. In a game against arch-rival North Carolina, Tim delivered a performance for the ages. He scored 25 points, grabbed 15 rebounds, and blocked 6 shots. The highlight reel from that game looked like a one-man show, with Tim swatting away shots and dominating both ends of the court. His performance cemented his status as the best player in college basketball and earned him the Naismith College Player of the Year award.

Throughout his time at Wake Forest, Tim developed a bond with the fans and the community. They saw him not just as a humble, hardworking individual who excels both on and off the court, beyond being a basketball player. His humility was legendary; he never sought the limelight, always deflecting praise to his teammates and coaches. Tim's unassuming nature endeared him to everyone who crossed his path, from fellow students to the janitors who cleaned the gym. Tim's college career culminated in his graduation in 1997. Unlike many athletes who leave college early for the lure of professional sports, Tim was determined to finish his degree. It was a promise he made to his mother, who had passed away before he finished high school. With diploma in hand, Tim had not only achieved his basketball dreams but had honored his family's values of education and perseverance.

After four stellar years at Wake Forest, Tim Duncan was ready for the next big step. By 1997, NBA scouts were practically camping outside his dorm room, eager to see the future star up close. The 1997 NBA Draft was approaching, and Tim was the undisputed number one pick. Even if he preferred blending into the background, the spotlight was firmly on him now. Tim, cool as a cucumber, didn't let any of the hype get to him. While others would be biting their nails off, Tim probably had his feet up, reading a psychology textbook. The San Antonio Spurs won the draft lottery and the right to pick first. The team was in desperate need of a game-changer, having come off a rough season plagued with injuries. Enter Tim Duncan, the perfect blend of talent, work ethic, and humility. The Spurs couldn't have scripted it better if they'd tried. On June 25, 1997, Tim Duncan was officially drafted as the first overall pick. The Big Fundamental was heading to Texas.

Arriving in San Antonio, Tim quickly formed a bond with Spurs' center and superstar, David Robinson. The Admiral, as Robinson was known, was a towering figure in more ways than one. Tim and David became the Twin Towers, a nickname that spoke to their formidable presence in the paint. Robinson, a future Hall of Famer, became both a mentor and a friend to Tim, helping him navigate the professional landscape while teaching him the intricacies of the NBA game. In his rookie season, Tim hit the ground running, averaging an impressive 21.1 points, 11.9 rebounds, and 2.5 blocks per game. His first game was against the Denver Nuggets, and from the opening tip, it was clear that Tim belonged. His footwork, honed from years of swimming and meticulous practice, baffled opponents. He moved with the grace of a ballet dancer and the power of a freight train. It didn't take long for Tim to collect accolades, and he was named the NBA Rookie of the Year in 1998. But Tim being Tim, took it all in stride, probably shrugging it off as no big deal. Tim's impact on the Spurs was immediate and profound. In his second season, the team finished with a 56-26 record, a dramatic turnaround from their previous struggles. The Spurs were no longer the underdogs; they were title contenders. Tim's partnership with David Robinson blossomed, and under the guidance of Coach Gregg Popovich, the team's strategy clicked perfectly. Popovich, known for his no-nonsense approach and dry wit, found a kindred spirit in Tim. Their mutual respect and understanding became a cornerstone of the Spurs' success.

The 1998-1999 season was a landmark year for Tim and the Spurs. It was a lockout-shortened season, but the Spurs were on a mission. Tim's consistency and dominance were key factors in the team's run to the playoffs. His performance in the postseason was, let's say... pretty nice. In the Western Conference Finals against the Portland Trail Blazers,

Tim averaged 20.8 points and 11.8 rebounds, leading the Spurs to their first-ever NBA Finals. In the Finals, the Spurs faced the New York Knicks. Tim's calm under pressure was legendary, and he delivered when it mattered most. He averaged 27.4 points and 14 rebounds per game in the series, dominating the Knicks' defense with his array of bank shots, hooks, and footwork that seemed almost magical. The Spurs won the series 4-1, clinching their first NBA Championship. Tim was named Finals MVP, cementing his status as one of the league's elite players. Off the court, Tim's life in San Antonio was as low-key as his personality. He eschewed the flashy lifestyle that many athletes embraced, preferring quiet nights with his family and teammates. He continued his pranks, keeping the locker room atmosphere light and fun. One famous prank involved filling teammate Malik Rose's car with popcorn. It took Malik hours to clean out the mess, and Tim's poker face never gave away the culprit. His sense of humor and down-to-earth nature made him beloved by teammates and fans alike.

Tim's early years in the NBA were defined by his relentless work ethic and desire to improve. He spent countless hours in the gym, fine-tuning his skills and conditioning. His approach to the game was methodical and almost scientific, breaking down his performance piece by piece to understand where he could get better. He studied his opponents meticulously, understanding their tendencies and devising ways to counter them. This cerebral approach, combined with his physical gifts, made Tim one of the most formidable players in the league.

The following seasons saw Tim continue to elevate his game and the Spurs' fortunes. His partnership with Robinson flourished until Robinson's retirement in 2003. Even then, Tim's leadership and consistency ensured that the Spurs remained competitive. His ability to adapt and grow with the team, embracing new roles and challenges, showcased his versatility and dedication. In these early NBA years, Tim Duncan laid the foundation for a career that would eventually be marked by numerous championships, MVP awards, and records. Yet, despite the accolades and the growing list of achievements, Tim remained the same humble, hardworking individual who started his journey on the beaches of Saint Croix. His transition from college to the NBA was seamless, marked by immediate success and the promise of even greater things to come.

Kobe Bryant

THE RISE OF A BASKETBALL ICON

Kobe Bryant's story begins with a flash of brilliance, like that unexpected moment when you finally find the matching sock after a week of searching. Born on August 23, 1978, in Philadelphia, Pennsylvania, Kobe Bean Bryant arrived on this planet with a name that screamed "destined for greatness." Seriously, "Bean" as a middle name? You can't make this stuff up. His dad, Joe "Jellybean" Bryant, was a professional basketball player, and his mom, Pamela Cox Bryant, was the secret sauce that held the family together. With Jellybean as a dad, basketball ran in Kobe's veins like the syrup on a stack of pancakes.

Kobe's early years were like a travel blog gone wild. When he was six, the family packed their bags and moved to Italy, where Joe continued his basketball career. Now, there's little Kobe, an energetic kid who speaks only English, suddenly landing in the country of pasta, soccer, and rapid-fire Italian. It was like being given a basketball and being told to dribble it on a tightrope. But hey, if Kobe could conquer the Italian language, what could he do on the basketball court! By the time he was fluent in Italian, he was already showing signs of basketball genius, practicing moves with a determination that would have made even Michelangelo proud. Back in the States, the Bryants moved to the Philadelphia suburb of Lower Merion. Kobe, now a high school freshman, was about to set the basketball world on fire like a pair of sneakers left too close to the campfire. Lower Merion High School hadn't seen such excitement since... well, ever. Kobe's arrival on the basketball team was like unleashing a superhero in a comic book. His freshman year was all about proving himself, and boy, did he prove himself. By the time he was a senior, Kobe had already racked up 2,883 points, smashing the Southeastern Pennsylvania record set by Wilt Chamberlain, another basketball legend.

Kobe's high school career was more than points and records. It was the story of a kid who approached basketball with the same seriousness that some people reserve for mastering the perfect skateboard trick. He'd spend hours in the gym, perfecting his shot, his dribble, his footwork. His dedication was like a relentless drumbeat, echoing through the halls of Lower Merion. His teammates often joked that Kobe practically lived in the gym. It was rumored that he had a secret cot tucked away behind the bleachers for late-night practice sessions. Kobe's standout performances caught the eye of NBA scouts faster than a pizza delivery guy on a Friday night. The buzz around him was electrifying. He had the charisma of a rock star and the skills of a seasoned pro. His highlight reels were like mini-action movies, featuring high-flying dunks, smooth-as-butter jump shots, and crossovers that left defenders tangled up like spaghetti. Colleges across the country were drooling at the prospect of having Kobe wear their jerseys, but Kobe had other plans. In 1996, in a move that shocked the basketball world, Kobe declared for the NBA draft straight out of high school. This was the kind of bold move that made people spit out their coffee in surprise. Skipping college wasn't unheard of, but it was rare. Kobe's confidence was unshakable. He knew he was ready for the big leagues, and he had the skills to back it up. And so, at the age of 17, Kobe entered the NBA draft, a decision that would change the course of basketball history forever.

The NBA draft day was like the Oscars for basketball nerds. The Charlotte Hornets picked Kobe 13th overall, but there was a twist in the plot. The Lakers, with their star-studded history and a knack for blockbuster moves, saw something special in Kobe. They pulled off a trade that sent Vlade Divac to the Hornets and brought Kobe to Los Angeles. It was like trading an old guitar for a shiny new rock star. And so, the stage was set. Kobe Bryant, the high school prodigy from Philadelphia with a globetrotting childhood and a relentless drive, was headed to Hollywood. The city of angels was about to witness the rise of a basketball phenomenon. The world was ready, the Lakers were ready, and most importantly, he was ready.

Kobe Bryant stepped into the spotlight of the NBA with the confidence of someone who had been preparing for this moment his entire life. At 17, Kobe was the youngest player in the NBA, a statistic that added an extra layer of excitement and scrutiny to his arrival. He was that teenager, not old enough to vote, driving to practice in a newly acquired luxury car, blending into a team of seasoned professionals who had mortgages, kids, and decades of experience. But Kobe's journey with the Lakers was not a smooth ride from the get-go; it was filled with challenges, growing pains, and moments of brilliance.

As a rookie, Kobe faced the uphill battle of proving himself in a league where rookies are often treated like the new kid in school – a bit of hazing, a lot of testing, and endless proving of worth. He came off the bench for most of his first season, which might sound less glamorous, but it was a crucial learning period. His minutes on the court were limited, and so were his opportunities to shine. Yet, even in those short bursts of playtime, Kobe showed glimpses of his future greatness. He had the kind of talent that was impossible to ignore, like trying to overlook an elephant in a living room. In his first year, he experienced a mix of stumbles, missteps, and air balls. Oh, the air balls! One of the most infamous moments came during the 1997 playoffs against the Utah Jazz. With the game on the line, Kobe took not one, not two, but four air ball shots. It was like watching a chef burn every dish in a cooking competition. But rather than being a setback, this experience forged Kobe's resilience. He took those missed shots as lessons, fueling his determination to improve. While some might have been disheartened, Kobe turned those air balls into a personal challenge, proving that what didn't kill you could indeed make you stronger.

The summer following his rookie season, Kobe was a fixture at the gym. He trained relentlessly, honing his skills and refining his game. His work ethic was legendary even at this early stage. Teammates would find him practicing hours before scheduled sessions, his face set in a mask of concentration. He aimed to be the best. And so, he approached training with a zeal that was part obsession, part passion, and all Kobe. As his second season began, Kobe's role with the Lakers started to expand. He was no longer the quiet rookie waiting for his chance. His minutes increased, and so did his contributions to the team. There were jaw-dropping dunks that defied gravity and defensive plays that showed his growing understanding of the game. Kobe's performance in the 1998 All-Star Game was a clear indicator of his rising star. He was the youngest player ever to start in an All-Star game, sharing the court with legends and holding his own with the confidence of someone who belonged.

Despite his individual achievements, Kobe was still a young player trying to fit into a team with established dynamics. The Lakers of the late '90s were a team in transition, with new players coming in and old ones leaving. Kobe's talent was undeniable, but he had to navigate the complexities of team politics, finding his place among more experienced players. It was during this time that his relationship with Shaquille O'Neal began to take shape. Shaq, the team's towering center and dominant force, had his own style and personality, which sometimes clashed with Kobe's intensity and drive. But beyond the locker room dramas and on-court rivalries, Kobe's second season was a testament to his growth and potential. He was evolving from a raw, talented teenager into a refined player who could change the course of a game. His confidence grew with each match, and his ability to perform under pressure became one of his defining traits. The kid from Lower Merion was no longer an NBA curiosity; he was becoming a bona fide star.

By the end of his second season, Kobe had earned his place in the NBA. He was a fan favorite, known for his electrifying plays and fearless attitude. Kids across the country were trying to mimic his moves, and the name "Kobe" was starting to echo in playgrounds and gymnasiums far beyond Los Angeles. The Lakers, with their eyes on future championships, knew they had a gem in Kobe. The team was beginning to mold itself around his potential, and Kobe was ready to lead, learn, and dominate. The path to greatness was set, and the NBA was watching. Kobe Bryant, the young star with a relentless drive and an insatiable thirst for success, was only getting started. The challenges of his rookie season had hardened him, and the successes of his second season had emboldened him. The stage was set for the rise of a basketball legend.

●

Kobe Bryant's journey from a promising rookie to a central figure in the Lakers' lineup was like watching a caterpillar morph into a butterfly, except this butterfly had a killer crossover and a deadly fadeaway jumper. By his third season, Kobe was no longer the new kid on the block; he was becoming the cornerstone of the Lakers' future. His transformation was both rapid and remarkable, marked by a work ethic that would make even the most diligent of ants look lazy. The 1998-1999 season was a turning point for Kobe. The NBA lockout shortened the season, but it didn't shorten Kobe's drive. This period was pivotal as Kobe continued to evolve, focusing not only on his physical game but also on his mental toughness. He became known for his relentless pursuit of perfection, spending countless hours studying game tapes, analyzing his moves, and strategizing ways to outsmart his opponents. His brain was as much a weapon as his body, and he wielded both with precision.

During this time, Kobe's partnership with Shaquille O'Neal began to truly flourish. On the court, they were a dynamic duo, like peanut butter and jelly or Batman and Robin, if Robin could dunk on anyone in sight. Shaq's dominant presence in the paint and Kobe's versatility and scoring ability made them an almost unstoppable force. However, this came with its share of drama. Their relationship is a roller coaster of highs and lows, full of brilliant moments and times of friction. They pushed each other, sometimes clashing, but ultimately they made each other better. Phil Jackson, the legendary coach known for his Zen-like approach and impressive resume, joined the Lakers in 1999. His arrival was like adding a master chef to a kitchen full of fresh ingredients. Jackson's coaching philosophy, centered around the triangle offense, was the perfect system to harness Kobe's skills and Shaq's power. Under Jackson's guidance, Kobe's game matured. He learned to balance his natural scoring instinct with the need to play within a team structure. It was like learning to play an instrument in an orchestra, where every note had to harmonize with the whole.

The 1999-2000 season was Kobe's true breakout. He started all 66 games he played in, averaging over 22 points per game, along with 6 rebounds and 4 assists. But statistics alone couldn't capture his impact. Kobe had become the Lakers' go-to guy in clutch situations, the player they turned to when the game was on the line. His ability to perform under pressure was becoming legendary. He hit game-winning shots, made crucial defensive plays, and seemed to thrive in the most intense moments. His style of play was electric, filled with acrobatic dunks, smooth jump shots, and tenacious defense. Kobe's dedication to his craft was evident in every aspect of his game. He was known to arrive at the practice facility before sunrise and stay long after his teammates had left. His commitment was like a beacon, guiding the team through tough stretches and inspiring everyone around him. Kobe's approach to basketball was holistic; he worked on his physical conditioning, his skills, and his mental game with equal fervor. He was a student of the sport, always looking for ways to improve, always hungry for the next challenge.

The culmination of all this hard work and synergy came in the 2000 NBA Finals. The Lakers faced the Indiana Pacers, and Kobe was ready to shine on the biggest stage of his career thus far. Although he sprained his ankle in Game 2 and had to sit out Game 3, he returned in Game 4 to deliver a performance for the ages. With Shaq fouled out, Kobe took over, scoring crucial points in overtime to lead the Lakers to a victory. His ability to step up in such a critical moment was a testament to his growth as a player and his unshakeable confidence. By the end of the series, the Lakers had secured their first championship in over a decade, and Kobe was a significant part of that success. At 21, he had transitioned from a promising talent to an NBA champion, a journey marked by relentless effort, remarkable talent, and an unwavering belief in himself. The celebration in Los Angeles was epic, with fans flooding the streets, and Kobe's name chanted with the kind of reverence reserved for true legends.

Kobe Bryant's ascent to stardom was a blend of raw talent, meticulous dedication, and an unyielding competitive spirit. His early years with the Lakers were a roller coaster of highs and lows, but through it all, Kobe's focus remained on becoming the best. He had set the stage for an illustrious career, filled with more challenges, triumphs, and moments that would leave an indelible mark on the world of basketball.

Michael Jordan

FROM PHENOM TO GLOBAL ICON

Listen up, today we're diving into the epic story of Michael Jordan. You might know him as the guy who could leap so high he might have had secret springs in his sneakers. But, before he was soaring above NBA courts and slam-dunking his way into history, he was a regular kid with a zest for life and a knack for sports.

Let's start with young Michael, born on February 17, 1963, in Brooklyn, New York. Yes, that's right, Brooklyn! Now, I know you must be thinking about the metropolis, busy roads, and tall structures... But don't get too attached to that picture because the Jordan family soon packed their bags and moved down south to Wilmington, North Carolina. Young Michael, wide-eyed, has a curiosity that could rival a detective on a hot case.

In Wilmington, Michael was part of a big family. He had four siblings: two older brothers, Larry and James Jr., an older sister, Deloris, and a younger sister, Roslyn. This household was buzzing with energy and competition, especially with those older brothers around. Imagine trying to grab the last piece of pie with a brother like Larry eyeing it! Michael had to learn early how to be quick, not just on his feet but with his hands too.

Now, you'd think with that competitive spirit, Michael would be all about basketball from the get-go, right? Wrong! Michael's first love was baseball. He played in Little League and dreamed of hitting home runs like his dad, James, who was a solid baseball player himself. But baseball wasn't the only game in town for young MJ. He was also pretty good at football, playing as a quarterback and showing off his arm with pinpoint passes. But then something happened that would change Michael's life forever: a basketball hoop appeared in his backyard. His older brother Larry would challenge him to one-on-one games, and boy, did those games get intense! Larry was taller and older, so naturally, he would win most of the time. However, instead of feeling defeated, Michael's competitive fire ignited. He vowed to get better, to work harder, and to eventually beat his brother.

The early days weren't all slam dunks and three-pointers. In fact, Michael often found himself outmatched. But he had something crucial: determination. Every loss against Larry was a lesson. He'd practice his dribbling, shooting, and defense, trying to figure out how to outsmart and outplay his older brother. And let me tell you, Larry wasn't taking it easy on him. These backyard games were like the NBA Finals for young Michael.

In school, Michael's athletic talent started to shine. At Ogden Elementary and later at Trask Junior High, he was involved in all sorts of sports activities. His PE teachers noticed his agility, his speed, and that competitive streak that made him never back down from a challenge. But sports aren't the only thing. Michael had to keep up with his studies too. His parents, Deloris and James, emphasized the importance of education. They believed in a well-rounded upbringing, where academics were just as important as athletics.

Around this time, Michael began to outgrow his shyness. He was known for his playful personality and sense of humor, often joking around with friends and family. He was the kind of kid who would pull pranks but also knew when to get serious, especially when it came to a game of basketball. The seeds of greatness were being planted, though nobody knew it yet. It's funny to think that the same kid who got beat by his brother every day would go on to become the greatest basketball player of all time. But that's the magic of hard work, determination, and a little bit of sibling rivalry.

Here's where the story gets really interesting. Michael Jordan, now a teenager, stepped into the halls of Emsley A. Laney High School in Wilmington, North Carolina. The year was 1978, and Michael was about to face one of the most talked-about moments in basketball lore. You see, even legends have humble beginnings and face challenges that make their victories even sweeter.

Michael, standing at about 5 feet 10 inches tall as a sophomore, decided to try out for the varsity basketball team. He had been working hard, practicing day and night, battling it out with Larry in the backyard. So, he thought, why not take this passion to the next level? He stepped onto that court, full of hope and dreams, expecting to make the team and showcase his talent. But life has a funny way of testing us, doesn't it? Michael didn't make the varsity team that year. Instead, he was placed on the junior varsity (JV) team. Now, for many kids, this would be a devastating blow. But for Michael, it was a spark that ignited an even fiercer determination. He took that disappointment and used it as fuel to propel him forward. This is where you see the heart of a champion—someone who doesn't give up when faced with setbacks but instead works harder to overcome them.

On the JV team, Michael Jordan became a star. He played with a chip on his shoulder, proving himself in every game. His skills started to blossom; his speed, agility, and basketball IQ were off the charts. He scored points in bunches, often leading his team to victory and making everyone take notice. Coaches, teammates, and even opposing players began to see that this kid had something special.

By the time his junior year rolled around, Michael had grown to about 6 feet 3 inches. He was now ready to conquer the varsity level. This time, there was no doubt—he made the varsity team and immediately became a standout player. His coach, Clifton "Pop" Herring, saw the potential in Michael and pushed him to develop his skills even further.

Michael was relentless in his pursuit of greatness, spending countless hours practicing his shots, honing his defense, and perfecting his overall game.

During his junior and senior years, Michael Jordan became the star of the Laney High Buccaneers. His explosive playing style, combined with his athleticism and sheer will to win, made him a formidable force on the court. He had an uncanny ability to read the game, anticipate his opponents' moves, and make dazzling plays that left spectators in awe. His dedication was unwavering; he practiced before school, after school, and any time he could find a hoop and a ball.

One particularly memorable game happened during his senior year, where he scored a staggering 40 points, leading his team to a crucial victory. The crowd erupted with every shot he made, and it was clear to everyone present that they were witnessing the rise of a future basketball legend. His performances earned him a spot in the McDonald's All-American Game, a prestigious showcase of the nation's top high school talent.

Despite his incredible high school career, Michael still faced skeptics. College recruiters were unsure if he had what it took to excel at the next level. But Michael had an unshakable confidence and a determination to prove them all wrong. His work ethic and competitive spirit were unmatched. He practiced tirelessly, studying the game and learning from every experience. He has a strong desire to be the best, surpassing mere goodness.

As his high school years came to a close, Michael Jordan had transformed from a young boy cut from the varsity team to a player who had colleges vying for his attention. He had grown both in height and in skill, becoming a dominant force on the basketball court. The disappointment of not making the varsity team as a sophomore had long been replaced by a string of triumphs that showcased his extraordinary talent and drive. This was just the beginning for Michael. His high school years were filled with highs and lows, but through it all, he showed an incredible resilience and an unwavering desire to succeed. Little did he know, the next chapter of his life would take him to the University of North Carolina, where he would continue to build his legacy. But for now, he was Michael Jordan, the high school star with dreams of greatness.

So, Michael Jordan's high school days were packed with lessons in perseverance and the raw power of determination. He had proven his mettle at Laney High, but the next stage was college basketball, and it was time for him to show the world what he could do. In 1981, Michael Jordan stepped onto the campus of the University of North Carolina at Chapel Hill, ready to take on a new set of challenges.

Playing for the Tar Heels under the legendary coach Dean Smith, Michael found himself in a program steeped in basketball tradition. Dean Smith was known for his emphasis on team play and discipline, and he saw the potential in young Michael. But even the greatest need refining, and Coach Smith worked diligently to hone Michael's skills, teaching him the finer points of the game and ensuring he developed a high basketball IQ.

In his freshman year, Michael made an immediate impact. He quickly became a key player for the Tar Heels, known for his athleticism, scoring ability, and defensive prowess. But it was one particular moment that cemented his place in college basketball history. In the 1982 NCAA Championship game against Georgetown, with just 15 seconds left on the clock and UNC down by one, the ball found its way to Michael. Calmly, he took a shot from the left wing, and as the ball soared through the air, the entire stadium held its breath. Swish! The ball went in, and the Tar Heels won the championship. That shot became known as "The Shot" and marked the beginning of Michael Jordan's ascent to basketball greatness.

Over the next two years at UNC, Michael continued to excel, earning accolades and showing the world his unmatched talent. He was named the College Player of the Year in both 1983 and 1984, and his performances were nothing short of spectacular. His time at UNC was a period of immense growth, both as a player and as a person, preparing him for the next monumental step: the NBA.

In 1984, Michael Jordan declared for the NBA Draft and was selected third overall by the Chicago Bulls. Now, entering the professional league, he was ready to make his mark. Right from his rookie season, Michael showcased his extraordinary skills, earning the NBA Rookie of the Year award. He dazzled fans with his scoring ability, high-flying dunks, and clutch performances. The Chicago Bulls, once a struggling team, suddenly had a beacon of hope.

Throughout the late 1980s, Michael continued to elevate his game. He became known for his incredible work ethic, often the first to arrive at practice and the last to leave. His athleticism was unparalleled, and he developed a signature move: the fadeaway jump shot. Opponents found it nearly impossible to guard him, as he could score from anywhere on the court. The phrase "Air Jordan" became synonymous with his ability to seemingly defy gravity, soaring through the air with elegance and power. His individual performances make him special, combined with his relentless drive to win. Michael led the Bulls to their first NBA Championship in 1991, defeating Magic Johnson and the Los Angeles Lakers. This victory was the start of something historic. The Bulls, under Michael's leadership, went on to win three consecutive championships, completing a first "three-peat" by 1993. Michael's competitiveness and will to win were unmatched, and he became known for his ability to perform under pressure, earning the nickname "His Airness."

In 1993, after achieving so much, Michael faced a personal tragedy with the loss of his father, James. This event led him to step away from basketball and pursue a brief career in professional baseball, a nod to his father's love for the sport. However, the pull of the basketball court was too strong to resist, and in March 1995, Michael made a dramatic return to the NBA, famously announcing his comeback with two words: "I'm back."

The Bulls, with Michael back in the lineup, were once again a force to be reckoned with. He led the team to another three consecutive championships from 1996 to 1998, solidifying his legacy as the greatest player of all time. His performances during these years were nothing short of legendary, including a game-winning shot against the Utah Jazz in the 1998 Finals, known as "The Last Shot." This shot secured his sixth NBA championship and his place in basketball immortality. Throughout his career, Michael Jordan's accolades were numerous: 14-time NBA All-Star, 10-time scoring champion, 5-time MVP, and 6-time NBA Finals MVP, among many others. But beyond the statistics and the awards, it was his sheer willpower, his relentless pursuit of excellence, and his ability to perform when it mattered most that defined him.

That's the story of Michael Jordan—from a determined youngster practicing in his backyard to a global icon who transformed the game of basketball. His journey teaches us that greatness comes not from avoiding challenges but from facing them head-on with perseverance and an unyielding spirit. And while Michael Jordan's career is filled with highlights and unforgettable moments, it is his relentless drive and love for the game that truly make him a legend.

Amazing Facts, Records, and Moments

Epic Basketball Blunders

Shaquille O'Neal's Free Throw Fiasco

Shaq, the giant of a man with a heart of gold, was known for many things: his dominant presence in the paint, his jovial personality, and, hilariously, his struggles at the free-throw line. There was one particular game where Shaq missed 11 consecutive free throws. Fans even started chanting, "Brick! Brick! Brick!" as he attempted to sink one. His average was so notoriously bad that teams developed the "Hack-a-Shaq" strategy, intentionally fouling him to force free throws.

JaVale McGee's Dunk Gone Wrong

JaVale McGee, known for his high-flying dunks and sometimes baffling plays, once attempted an ambitious self-alley-oop from beyond the three-point line. He tossed the ball off the backboard, ran to catch it, and then spectacularly completed the dunk. However, given that his team was trailing, the move was seen as ill-timed showboating. His coach's expression was a mix of disbelief and exasperation. This play secured McGee a frequent spot on Shaqtin' a Fool, a segment highlighting the NBA's funniest moments.

Chris Webber's Infamous Timeout

Back in the 1993 NCAA Championship game, Chris Webber, a star for the University of Michigan, called a timeout with seconds left on the clock. The only problem? His team had no timeouts left. This resulted in a technical foul and the other team getting free throws and possession, costing Michigan the game. It's a mistake that's haunted Webber for years, but it's also one that basketball fans will never forget.

DeAndre Jordan's Missed Dunk

During a game with the Los Angeles Clippers, DeAndre Jordan had an open path to the basket for a dunk. He went up with all the power in the world, but the ball hit the back of the rim and flew back out. It was a surprising missed opportunity that left both fans and teammates in disbelief. His teammates' reactions ranged from surprise to amusement, underscoring the unpredictable nature of live sports.

Metta World Peace's (Ron Artest) Quirky Moment

Metta World Peace, formerly known as Ron Artest, is no stranger to on-court antics. During a game, he once humorously thanked his psychiatrist in a post-game interview after the Los Angeles Lakers won the 2010 NBA Championship. His candid and unexpected acknowledgment showcased his unique personality and provided a memorable moment for fans.

Nick Young's Premature Celebration

Swaggy P, aka Nick Young, is no stranger to confidence. During one game, he shot a three-pointer and, thinking it was a sure thing, turned around and celebrated with his signature swagger. Little did he know, the ball clanked off the rim and missed entirely. The slow-motion replay of his confident strut turning into bewilderment is a staple in NBA blooper reels.

Jason Kidd's Soda Spill Strategy

When coaching the Brooklyn Nets, Jason Kidd famously (or infamously) spilled a cup of soda on the court to buy his team extra time. With no timeouts left, Kidd subtly told his player to "hit me," and the collision sent soda flying everywhere, forcing the referees to clean up the mess and giving his team a breather. The tactic was clever but blatantly obvious, leading to a fine and a lot of laughs.

Michael Ruffin's Premature Throw

In a 2007 game, the Washington Wizards were up by three points with seconds to go. Michael Ruffin, thinking the game was over, grabbed a rebound and heaved the ball high into the air to run out the clock. But the ball came down quickly, and the opposing team, the Toronto Raptors, caught it and made a three-pointer to send the game into over-time. The Wizards ended up losing in overtime, making Ruffin's throw a monumental blunder.

Delonte West's Forgotten Play

Delonte West once had a memorable moment when he kissed his teammate on the cheek during a game, leading to laughter and surprise, it highlighted a humorous side of his personality and added to his repertoire of amusing on-court moments

Gerald Green's Dunk Malfunction

Known for his incredible dunking ability, Gerald Green had a memorable moment during the 2013 NBA Slam Dunk Contest. While attempting a between-the-legs dunk, he successfully executed the move but missed the dunk after the ball hit the back rim. This rare misstep in front of a national audience was a reminder that even the most talented dunkers can have off moments, adding to the suspense and excitement of the contest.

Dunk Legends: Gravity-Defying Feats

Spud Webb's Slam Dunk Contest Victory (1986)

Let's start with one of the most mind-blowing, gravity-defying moments in basketball history. Standing at a mere 5'7", Spud Webb stunned the world when he won the NBA Slam Dunk Contest in 1986. Webb's height was considered a disadvantage, but he used it to his benefit by performing dunks that made fans and judges' jaws drop. His most famous dunks included a reverse two-handed dunk and a double-pump reverse dunk, which showcased his incredible leaping ability and agility. Webb's win proved that size doesn't matter when you have the heart and hops to back it up.

Michael Jordan's Free-Throw Line Dunk (1988)

Michael Jordan, often called the greatest basketball player of all time, cemented his legacy with his iconic free-throw line dunk during the 1988 Slam Dunk Contest. Taking off from the free-throw line, Jordan seemed to defy gravity as he soared through the air, his tongue out in classic MJ fashion. This dunk became an indelible image of basketball excellence and athletic prowess, symbolizing the peak of Jordan's high-flying career.

Vince Carter's Dunk (2000 Olympics)

Vince Carter, known for his explosive dunks, delivered one of the most outrageous slams during the 2000 Sydney Olympics. In a game against France, Carter stole the ball and, with a head full of steam, leaped over 7'2" center Frédéric Weis, dunking the ball with authority. This feat was dubbed the "Dunk of Death" and is widely regarded as one of the most incredible dunks in the history of the sport, showcasing Carter's unreal athleticism.

Blake Griffin Jumps Over a Car (2011)

During the 2011 NBA Slam Dunk Contest, Blake Griffin pulled off a stunt that left the audience in awe. He leaped over the hood of a Kia Optima, caught a lob from Baron Davis, and dunked the ball, all while the car's horn blared in the background. The sheer spectacle of a player jumping over a car made this dunk one for the ages, highlighting Griffin's explosive power and creativity.

Shaquille O'Neal Breaks the Backboard (1992-1993)

Shaquille O'Neal, known for his massive size and strength, caused a stir when he shattered the backboard twice during his rookie season in the NBA. The most famous instance occurred in a game against the New Jersey Nets in 1993, where the force of Shaq's dunk brought the entire basket structure down, causing a delay in the game. This moment underscored Shaq's dominance and left an indelible mark on basketball history, prompting the NBA to reinforce backboards to prevent future breakages.

Dominique Wilkins' Windmill Dunk (1985)

Dominique Wilkins, known as the "Human Highlight Film," was a dunking machine. One of his most memorable dunks came during the 1985 Slam Dunk Contest, where he executed a powerful windmill dunk that showcased his strength, agility, and flair. Wilkins' windmill became a signature move and a staple in dunk contests for years to come, earning him a place among the all-time greats in dunking history.

LeBron James' Alley-Oop Off the Backboard (2013)

In a regular-season game against the Atlanta Hawks in February 2013, LeBron James executed one of the most impressive alley-oop dunks ever seen. Dwyane Wade stole a pass, ran down the sideline, and threw the ball off the backboard. LeBron, sprinting down the court, caught it mid-air and slammed it home with ferocity. The timing, coordination, and sheer athleticism displayed in this play left fans and players alike in sheer disbelief. This play became one of the defining highlights of the Wade-LeBron duo during their time with the Miami Heat

Julius Erving's Baseline Scoop Layup (1980)

Julius "Dr. J" Erving was a pioneer of the modern dunk. One of his most legendary moves occurred during Game 4 of the 1980 NBA Finals against the Los Angeles Lakers. Dr. J drove baseline, cradled the ball in one hand, and soared under the backboard before scooping the ball up and performing a reverse layup on the other side. This move, known as the "Baseline Scoop," showcased Erving's creativity and grace, setting a new standard for aerial artistry.

Aaron Gordon's Under-the-Legs Dunk (2016)

In the 2016 Slam Dunk Contest, Aaron Gordon delivered a dunk that many consider one of the greatest ever. Using the Orlando Magic's mascot, Stuff the Magic Dragon, as a prop, Gordon jumped over the mascot, caught the ball under his legs, and dunked it with authority. The combination of innovation, difficulty, and execution made this dunk an instant classic, earning Gordon widespread acclaim despite narrowly losing the contest.

Zach LaVine's Between-the-Legs Free-Throw Line Dunk (2016)

Zach LaVine, known for his dunking prowess, took the 2016 Slam Dunk Contest by storm with a series of jaw-dropping slams. His most remarkable dunk involved taking off from just inside the free-throw line and going between his legs before dunking the ball. This blend of power, finesse, and difficulty solidified LaVine's reputation as one of the best dunkers of his generation, leaving fans and judges in utter disbelief.

Hoops in Space: Galactic Basketball Adventures

Space Jam: The Ultimate Crossover

In 1996, the world was blessed with "Space Jam," a movie where the legendary Michael Jordan teamed up with Bugs Bunny and the Looney Tunes gang to battle evil space aliens in a high-stakes basketball game. The film became an instant classic, blending the real-world prowess of Jordan with the wacky antics of animated characters, all under the threat of alien domination. This quirky, and fun crossover has since become a cultural icon.

Astronaut Hoops: Dunking in Zero Gravity

In 2019, astronauts aboard the International Space Station (ISS) celebrated their mission milestones with various recreational activities. They have been known to engage in activities such as playing with a basketball, soccer ball, demonstrating the unique challenges and fun of sports in zero gravity. The footage of astronauts enjoying these moments highlights the lighter side of life aboard the ISS and the innovative ways they find to relax and have fun.

Kareem Abdul-Jabbar's Cinematic Cameo

Kareem Abdul-Jabbar, one of the greatest basketball players of all time, is also known for his cameo in the 1980 comedy film "Airplane!" where he played Roger Murdock, a co-pilot. This role showcased his acting skills and sense of humor, adding a memorable twist to his illustrious basketball career. His appearance in "Airplane!" remains a beloved moment in film history.

Space Age Sneakers: Nike's Galactic Inspiration

In 2012, Nike released the "Galaxy" pack of sneakers during the NBA All-Star Weekend. This collection featured space-themed designs with starry patterns, glow-in-the-dark soles, and galaxy-inspired colorways. The sneakers became a massive hit, blending the allure of space with the culture of basketball footwear, making them highly sought after by sneakerheads and basketball fans alike.

Shaq's Astronaut Dreams

Shaquille O'Neal, known for his larger-than-life personality and dominant basketball career, has often expressed interest in science and technology, showcasing his curiosity beyond basketball. Though he chose the path of a basketball legend instead, Shaq's fascination with space has never waned. He often jokes about how he would have been the biggest astronaut ever, bringing his unique brand of humor to the cosmos.

Houston Rockets: A Galactic Connection

The Houston Rockets, an NBA team, have a natural connection to space due to their home city's role in the U.S. space program. Houston is home to NASA's Johnson Space Center, and the team's name and logo reflect this cosmic connection. The Rockets have embraced this identity, often incorporating space themes into their branding and marketing, strengthening the bond between basketball and space exploration.

Red Bull's King of the Rock Tournament

In 2011, Red Bull created the "King of the Rock" tournament, a 1-on-1 basketball competition held at the historic Alcatraz Island. While not involving high-altitude adventure, this unique setting captured imaginations by combining the excitement of basketball with the eerie, dramatic backdrop of the former prison. The event highlighted how unconventional venues could add a new dimension to the sport.

Steph Curry's Moon Landing Controversy

In 2018, Stephen Curry, the sharpshooting star of the Golden State Warriors, sparked a playful controversy when he jokingly questioned the moon landing during a podcast. NASA quickly invited him to tour the Johnson Space Center to see the moon rocks and learn more about the Apollo missions. Curry accepted the invitation, and the incident highlighted how basketball stars can influence public interest in space exploration.

Mars Missions: NASA's Aspirations

While NASA has not proposed setting up a basketball hoop on Mars directly, they have continuously aimed to make space exploration relatable and engaging to the public. Initiatives like the "Send Your Name to Mars" campaign and educational outreach programs inspire the next generation of space enthusiasts. NASA's creative efforts to engage the public remind us that the possibilities in space exploration are limitless. Imagine a slam dunk with Mars's lower gravity—players would soar higher than ever before!

Dennis Rodman: The Intergalactic Diplomat

Dennis Rodman, a basketball player known for his colorful personality and rebounding prowess, has ventured into the realm of international diplomacy, befriending North Korean leader Kim Jong-un. This unusual friendship has garnered significant media attention and added an unexpected chapter to Rodman's life. His diplomatic efforts reflect his unpredictable and incredible persona, making headlines worldwide.

Mascot Mayhem: The Wildest Court Mascots

Benny the Bull (Chicago Bulls)

Benny the Bull is the ultimate prankster and showman. One of his most infamous stunts was when he took a giant popcorn container and, in true Benny style, dumped it over an unsuspecting fan, showering them with popcorn. Benny's antics don't stop there; he's also known for his wild dance moves, trampoline dunks, and his hilarious "kiss cam" pranks where he plants big smooches on fans, much to their surprise!

The Raptor (Toronto Raptors)

The Raptor is a dynamo of energy and humor. One legendary moment was when he dressed in an inflatable T-Rex costume and hilariously tried to perform dunks, wobbling and bouncing around the court. Another unforgettable incident was when he attempted to slide down a flight of stairs on his tail during a game, leading to a comical and slightly embarrassing tumble that left fans roaring with laughter.

Stuff the Magic Dragon (Orlando Magic)

Stuff is always up for a good laugh. In one memorable game, he proposed to a fan in a grand romantic gesture complete with a huge ring and a serenade. Another time, Stuff brought the magic by performing a skit as a wizard—complete with a fog machine and dramatic lights—and flew around the court on a zipline, leaving fans in awe of his theatrical flair.

Gritty (Philadelphia Flyers)

Gritty, the beloved yet chaotic mascot of the Philadelphia Flyers, is renowned for his over-the-top antics in the NHL. Known for riding tricycles around the ice and engaging in playful mischief, Gritty's antics include everything from pie-throwing contests with fans to mock wrestling matches, solidifying his reputation as a mascot who knows no bounds.

Bango the Buck (Milwaukee Bucks)

Bango is a daredevil mascot with a knack for high-flying stunts. One of his most jaw-dropping performances involved climbing a 16-foot ladder, balancing precariously, and then executing a perfect backflip dunk. Bango's love for dramatic entrances is well-known, such as the time he rappelled from the ceiling of the arena, surprising everyone and earning thunderous applause.

Pierre the Pelican (New Orleans Pelicans)

Pierre the Pelican has a flair for the theatrical. During Mardi Gras season, he once led a second-line parade through the stands, complete with a brass band and bead-throwing, turning a regular game into a carnival. Pierre's comedic timing is impeccable, like the time he pretended to faint dramatically after a referee's questionable call, leaving fans in stitches.

Rocky the Mountain Lion (Denver Nuggets)

Rocky is a master of slapstick humor and daring stunts. One of his most famous antics was when he rappelled from the ceiling to make a grand entrance at center court. Rocky also loves a good prank; he once sneaked up behind a fan and sprayed them with silly string, much to the delight of the audience.

The Gorilla (Phoenix Suns)

The Gorilla has been entertaining Suns fans with his acrobatic dunks and slapstick humor for decades. In a particularly memorable moment, Go dressed up as Elvis Presley and performed a series of acrobatic stunts while lip-syncing to "Jailhouse Rock." Another time, he joined the Suns' dance team in a hilariously out-of-sync routine that had the entire arena laughing.

Moondog (Cleveland Cavaliers)

Moondog is known for his unpredictable and humorous antics. He once rode a miniature motorcycle around the court, avoiding collisions with players and officials, much to the crowd's amusement. Moondog also loves interacting with fans, such as the time he "stole" a fan's popcorn and then tossed it into the air, creating a popcorn shower that had everyone laughing.

Hooper (Detroit Pistons)

Hooper's wildest stunt involved dressing up as a referee and hilariously mimicking the officials' calls and gestures, entertaining the crowd. In another unforgettable moment, Hooper orchestrated a flash mob in the middle of a game, leading fans and dancers in a surprise choreographed routine that had everyone on their feet and cheering.

Animal Invasions: When Wildlife Takes the Court

Manu Ginobili vs. The Bat

2009, a San Antonio Spurs game. Everything's going smoothly until—bam! A bat swoops down, thinking it's the newest draft pick. The crowd goes nuts, the players freeze, and then Manu Ginobili, channeling his inner Batman, swats the bat out of mid-air with his bare hand! Imagine the bat thinking, "Hey, I was just trying to join the team!" Manu instantly became not just a basketball hero, but a superhero. And yes, he did get a rabies shot, because even superheroes have to follow safety protocols!

The Toronto Raptor's Mascot Gets Upstaged

The Toronto Raptor's Mascot Gets Upstaged "In 2013, during a Toronto Raptors game, the team's mascot was temporarily upstaged by a squirrel. This little daredevil dashed through the stands and onto the court, stealing the show from the official mascot. Imagine the mascot thinking, 'Hey, that's my job!' The squirrel scurried through the stands, evading capture like it was training for the Olympics, giving fans a hilarious halftime show before finally being caught.

The 2019 Bat at Sacramento State

There was a 2019 college game between Sacramento State and Northern Arizona University. Mid-game, a bat swooped down fluttered into the arena, causing a brief disruption. Players and referees paused as staff worked to safely guide the bat out of the building. It added a surprising and slightly spooky twist to the game.

Outdoor Games and Nature's Surprises

At the Venice Beach courts in California, seagulls often make unexpected cameos. One day, a player's hotdog became the target of a seagull's daring heist. The bird swooped down, snatched the hotdog right out of his hand, and flew off like it was in an action movie. The player's stunned face and the gull's triumphant escape had everyone in stitches.

Goat Invasion at a Greek League Game

Imagine a basketball game in Greece suddenly being interrupted by a goat. This curious critter ambled onto the court, looking like it wanted to join the team. Players and referees tried to herd the goat away, but it seemed more interested in checking out the action. Eventually, they managed to escort the goat out, but not before it gave everyone a story for the ages.

Pigeon Problems in Indiana

During a Pacers game in Indiana, a pigeon managed to get into the arena and began flying around the court. The bird caused several delays as it swooped low over the players' heads, like it was trying to get a bird's-eye view of the game. Attempts to shoo it away only made things more chaotic, and it took quite a while before the pigeon was finally ushered out. It was like an impromptu bird show right in the middle of the game.

Cricket Intrusion at a High School Game

In Texas, a high school basketball game turned into a cricket fest when a swarm of crickets flooded the gym. The bright lights attracted the insects, which then covered the court, making players slip and slide as they tried to play. The game was paused as everyone worked together to sweep the crickets off the court, turning a regular game into an unforgettable, albeit buggy, experience.

Ancient Hoops: Historic Games that Shaped Basketball

Mesoamerican Ballgame (Ullamaliztli)

Dating back to around 1400 BCE, the Mesoamerican ballgame was a prominent ritual and sport among the Olmecs, Maya, and Aztecs. It symbolized cosmic battles between light and dark, life and death, serving as a key element in religious and societal life. The courts, known as "tlachtli" or "pok-ta-pok," were sacred spaces. Players used only their hips, forearms, and thighs to keep a heavy rubber ball in play, attempting to pass it through a vertical stone hoop mounted high on the court walls. These courts were large, often with towering walls, and varied in size across regions. Scoring through the hoop was rare and held significant importance, as the games often carried ritual significance, with stakes ranging from divine favor to, in some cases, human sacrifice. **Influence on Basketball**: While the Mesoamerican ballgame and basketball evolved independently, they share notable similarities. Both games involve teamwork, strategic passing, and the objective of scoring by getting a ball through a hoop. The precision and skill required in the Mesoamerican game, especially with the high placement of the hoop, bear some resemblance to the shooting techniques in basketball. However, basketball as we know it developed separately in the 19th century, with its own distinct rules and cultural context

Episkyros

Episkyros was the ancient Greeks' game around 800 BCE, part of their athletic tradition and festival fun. This game was rough and tough, with lots of physical contact. Played on a rectangular field marked by a central line, two teams (usually 12-14 players each) tried to throw a ball over the heads of their opponents to score points. It was all about passing and outsmarting the other team. **Influence on Basketball**: Episkyros's strategic passing and teamwork are mirrored in basketball's gameplay. The goal of advancing the ball and scoring points echoes basketball's aim of getting the ball into the hoop.

Harpastum

From around 100 BCE to 400 CE, the Romans played Harpastum. It was a soldier's game, keeping them fit and ready for action. Played on a rectangular field, two teams battled to keep a small, hard ball and score by getting it over the opponents' lines. Any body part could move the ball, and the game was a physical contest of endurance, speed, and strategy. **Influence on Basketball**: Harpastum's focus on ball control, possession, and strategic teamwork parallels basketball's principles of dribbling, passing, and coordinated team maneuvers. The competitive nature and goal-oriented objectives are foundational to basketball.

Ulama

Ulama is a traditional game still played in parts of Mexico today, with roots in ancient Mesoamerican ballgames. Preserving cultural heritage, Ulama is played at festivals and community events. Players use their hips, forearms, or paddles to hit a solid rubber ball, aiming to pass it through a hoop or into specific court areas. Teams or singles can play, with varied rules and scoring. **Influence on Basketball**: Ulama's ball handling and accuracy influenced basketball's focus on precision and skill in making baskets. The teamwork and strategy elements are reflected in basketball's offensive and defensive play.

Chunkey

Chunkey, played by Native American tribes like the Cherokee from at least 600 CE, was both recreational and ceremonial. Players rolled a stone disk and threw spears to land as close to the stopped disk as possible, requiring precision and accuracy. **Influence on Basketball**: Chunkey's emphasis on precision and competition is reflected in basketball's shooting aspects, where accurate aiming and scoring are crucial. The competitive nature and skill in aiming influenced basketball's precision-based scoring.

Pallone col Bracciale

Popular in Italy during the 16th and 17th centuries, Pallone col Bracciale required skill and agility. Players wore a wooden gauntlet called a 'bracciale' to strike a ball in mid-air, aiming to keep it in play over a net or within a defined court. Teams scored points by landing the ball in the opponent's court, using strategic placement and power **Influence on Basketball**: The skill and precision required in Pallone col Bracciale, particularly in hitting a moving target with power and control, resemble the techniques used in basketball shooting. Both sports emphasize competitive play and teamwork, though they evolved independently without a direct historical connection.

Mob Football

Played in medieval Europe, especially England, from the 12th century, Mob Football was chaotic and unstructured. Entire villages moved a ball to a goal through streets and fields, with few rules and lots of physical contact and tackling. **Influence on Basketball**: Mob Football introduced team-based, goal-oriented games. Advancing a ball toward a target underlies many modern team sports, including basketball. The teamwork and strategy in reaching the goal are foundational to basketball's structure.

The Hidden Stars of Basketball

Ah, basketball – the game that turns sneakers into jet engines and hardwood floors into launch pads for dreams. You might know the legends: Michael Jordan with his gravity-defying leaps, LeBron James with his herculean strength, and Magic Johnson with his no-look passes that made defenders dizzy. But let's shine a spotlight on some unsung heroes who've been quietly shaking up the world of basketball like secret agents in high-tops. These ten players and pioneers might not be household names, but their stories are pure gold and worthy of a standing ovation.

Lusia Harris: The Queen Who Dared to Dream

Lusia Harris is a name that should echo in the halls of basketball history, perhaps with a megaphone! She scored the first points in Olympic women's basketball in 1976, putting her stamp on the game with a slam dunk of authority. But wait, it gets even better – she was one of the very few women ever drafted by an NBA team! In 1977, the New Orleans Jazz selected her in the seventh round. Although she didn't play in the NBA, Harris paved the way for future generations of female ballers, leaving her size 12 sneakers as big shoes to fill. And here's a fun fact to add some bounce to your step: while Denise Long was also drafted by the NBA, her selection was voided, making Harris the first and only woman officially drafted by an NBA team. Thank you Harris!

Manute Bol: The Shot-Blocking Giraffe

Manute Bol, standing at an astonishing 7 feet 7 inches, was a towering presence on the court, like a basketball-playing giraffe! Known for his remarkable shot-blocking ability, Bol was a player who could change the course of a game with his defense – swatting shots away like pesky flies. Off the court, Bol was equally heroic, dedicating his life and much of his fortune to humanitarian efforts in his native Sudan. While there are many tall tales about his shot-blocking prowess, specific claims like blocking four consecutive shots in a single possession require credible sources to be verified. Nonetheless, his impact both on and off the court remains as indisputable as the height of his game

Muggsy Bogues: The David in the Land of Goliaths

Standing at just 5 feet 3 inches, Tyrone "Muggsy" Bogues defied all odds to become an NBA star. While most players were looking down at him, Bogues was busy dribbling circles around them and dishing out assists like a magician pulling rabbits out of hats. His career is a testament to the fact that heart and hustle can overshadow height any day.

Cheryl Miller: The Unstoppable Force

Cheryl Miller might be best known as the sister of NBA legend Reggie Miller, but don't get it twisted – Cheryl's game was unparalleled. In high school, she scored 105 points in a single game. Yes, you read that right – 105 points! She went on to dominate college basketball and was a key figure in pushing women's basketball into the spotlight. Her relentless drive and jaw-dropping skill set make her one of the greatest players, period.

Nancy Lieberman: The Lady Magic

Nancy Lieberman, often dubbed "Lady Magic," was a trailblazer in women's basketball. Her court vision and playmaking ability were so extraordinary that she became the first woman to play in a men's professional basketball league, the USBL. Lieberman later transitioned into coaching and broadcasting, proving that her basketball IQ was off the charts.

Earl Lloyd: The Quiet Trailblazer

Earl Lloyd broke the NBA color barrier in 1950, becoming the first African American to play in an NBA game. His impact wasn't loud and flashy but steady and powerful, paving the way for future generations of players. Lloyd's career is a reminder that sometimes, the biggest changes come from those who walk softly but carry a big stick – or in this case, a basketball.

Becky Hammon: The Coach Who Could

Becky Hammon, undrafted and initially overlooked, carved out an illustrious career in the WNBA with her sharpshooting and basketball savvy. But her story didn't end there. Hammon broke another barrier by becoming the first full-time female assistant coach in the NBA with the San Antonio Spurs. She's a pioneer, proving that with enough grit and determination, you can rewrite the playbook.

Spud Webb: The Dunking Dynamo

Anthony "Spud" Webb, another pint-sized powerhouse at 5 feet 7 inches, stunned the basketball world when he won the 1986 NBA Slam Dunk Contest. His vertical leap was so explosive, it seemed like he had springs in his sneakers. Webb's victory defied the notion that height determines athleticism, proving that skill and determination can overcome physical limitations.

Teresa Weatherspoon: The Shot Heard 'Round the World

Teresa Weatherspoon, a dynamo in women's basketball, is best remembered for "The Shot" – a miraculous, half-court buzzer-beater in the 1999 WNBA Finals that sent the series to a deciding game. Beyond her clutch shooting, Weatherspoon was known for her leadership and defensive prowess, earning her a spot in the Women's Basketball Hall of Fame.

Don Barksdale: The Barrier Breaker

Don Barksdale was the first African American to be named an NCAA All-American and the first to play on a U.S. Olympic basketball team, winning gold in 1948. Barksdale's journey didn't stop there – he became the first African American to play in an NBA All-Star Game in 1953. His legacy is a testament to breaking barriers and challenging the status quo.

Odd Rituals and Lucky Charms

Michael Jordan's Lucky North Carolina Shorts

The GOAT himself, Michael Jordan, had a superstition that's become the stuff of legends. Jordan wore his University of North Carolina practice shorts under his Chicago Bulls uniform for good luck. He believed these shorts brought him luck and a piece of his alma mater's winning spirit. It's as if he was channeling the power of his college days with every slam dunk and fadeaway jumper.

Jason Terry's Pre-Game Shorts

Known for his eccentric habits, Jason Terry had a ritual that was sartorially unique. Before each game, he had a unique habit—he wore the opposing team's shorts the night before a game. Talk about getting into the enemy's head! It's a wonder he didn't have nightmares of getting dunked on.

LeBron James' Powder Toss

LeBron James' iconic chalk toss is one of the most recognizable pre-game rituals in basketball. Before every game, King James would grab some chalk powder, toss it in the air, and let it rain down like magical fairy dust. This ritual, which started during his first stint with the Cleveland Cavaliers, was his way of getting in the zone and electrifying the crowd.

Kevin Garnett's Headbutts

If you've ever seen Kevin Garnett in action, you know he's a ball of intense energy. To psych himself up before games, Garnett would headbutt the padding of the basket stanchion. Yep, you read that right. This fierce ritual was a way for him to channel his inner beast mode, ready to dominate both ends of the floor.

Russell Westbrook's Dance Routine

Known for his explosive style of play, Russell Westbrook also brings flair and energy to the game even before tip-off. His pre-game ritual often includes an elaborate, high-energy dance routine with former teammate Cameron Payne, blending rhythm and intensity. Far from just showmanship, these routines became an iconic part of Westbrook's preparation during his time with the Oklahoma City Thunder. The routines, which pumped up both the team and fans, reflected Westbrook's dynamic personality and passion for the game. Notably, these dances sometimes sparked rival interactions, as opponents occasionally attempted to disrupt the ritual, underscoring how much it was part of Westbrook's mental and physical warm-up

Stephen Curry's Rigorous Shooting Routine

Known for his sharpshooting prowess, Stephen Curry goes through a meticulous pre-game shooting routine. Before every game, Curry completes an extensive warm-up session, making shots from all over the court, including long-range three-pointers and unique trick shots. This routine sharpens his focus and ensures he's in peak form to dominate the game.

Karl Malone's Pre-Game Ritual

The Mailman always delivered, and part of his pre-game ritual involved some distinct routines. Karl Malone would eat a chicken meal and listen to country music to get into the right mindset before games. This routine was his way of showing respect and readiness for the game he loved.

Cutting-Edge Basketball Innovations

Smart Basketballs

Companies like Wilson and Spalding have developed smart basketballs equipped with embedded sensors that track data on every dribble, pass, and shot. These basketballs can connect to your smartphone via Bluetooth, providing real-time analytics on your shooting arc, release speed, and dribbling intensity. For instance, the Wilson X Connected Basketball tracks your shot attempts and makes, offering feedback to improve your game. It's like having a miniature coach inside the ball, yelling, "Bend your knees more!" every time you shoot.

Wearable Tech

Modern athletes are donning more than just jerseys and shorts; they're now equipped with smart apparel. Devices like the Catapult Vector and WHOOP straps provide comprehensive data on players' biomechanics, heart rate, and exertion levels. These wearables monitor how much force you use to jump, how fast you sprint, and even your recovery times. Imagine your jersey telling you to cool down because you're about to overexert yourself. It's like having your mom and coach in one piece of clothing, nagging you to take care of yourself.

High-Speed Cameras and Motion Capture

Traditional cameras can't capture the lightning-fast movements of modern basketball players. That's where high-speed cameras and motion capture systems come in, like those used by NBA teams for in-depth analysis. Systems such as SportVU and Kinexon track every movement in millisecond detail, allowing for precise breakdowns of shooting forms, defensive stances, and more. It's like having The Matrix's bullet time technology to analyze whether you really did travel on that last play.

Smart Courts

Basketball courts are getting an IQ boost with embedded technology. Smart courts, like those developed by Nike and SportVU, come equipped with sensors and cameras that track the ball and players in real time. These courts can generate live statistics, heat maps, and performance analyses instantly. Imagine a court that knows exactly where you missed that three-pointer and can tell you how to correct your form. It's like the floor itself is your coach, whispering advice under your feet.

Biomechanics Analysis

Understanding how the body moves is crucial for peak performance. Biomechanics analysis uses advanced motion sensors and cameras to capture and study players' movements in exhaustive detail. Systems like Dartfish and Kinovea break down every aspect of a player's motion, from joint angles to muscle activation. This data helps in creating personalized training regimens that optimize performance and prevent injuries. It's like having a high-tech physiotherapist that can see inside your body and tweak your jump shot just right.

Wearable Injury Prevention Devices

Staying injury-free is vital for any athlete, and wearable tech is stepping up to keep players safe. Devices like the Motus Sleeve and the Hyperice Vyper monitor stress levels on muscles and joints, alerting players and coaches to potential injury risks before they become serious. These gadgets can tell if you're overworking a muscle or if your joints are taking too much strain, helping you avoid those dreaded injuries. It's like having a personal medical team monitoring you around the clock, ensuring you stay in peak condition.

Basketball Brain Games And Trivia!

Game 1 – Basketball Rules Trivia Challenge

Are you ready to test your knowledge of basketball regulations? Each question will challenge your understanding of the game's rules, from fouls to scoring, and more. Hints will guide you along the way. Let's dive in!

Question 1:
What is the maximum amount of time an offensive player can hold the ball without dribbling, passing, or shooting if they are closely guarded?

A) 3 seconds
B) 5 seconds
C) 10 seconds
D) 24 seconds

Question 2:
How many personal fouls in the NBA does a player need to accumulate before being disqualified from the game?

A) 4 fouls
B) 5 fouls
C) 6 fouls
D) 7 fouls

Question 3:
Which of the following is considered a traveling violation?

A) Moving your pivot foot after stopping your dribble
B) Dribbling the ball above your waist

C) Passing the ball without looking at the recipient

D) Blocking a shot with both hands

Question 4:
How long can a defensive player stay in the paint (key) without actively guarding an opponent?

A) 2 seconds

B) 3 seconds

C) 5 seconds

D) 10 seconds

Question 5:
What is the rule regarding the number of steps a player can take after stopping their dribble?

A) 1 step

B) 2 steps

C) 3 steps

D) 4 steps

Question 6:
How many points is a basket worth if the shooter is standing behind the three-point line when they release the ball?

A) 1 point

B) 2 points

C) 3 points

D) 4 points

Question 7:
When does the shot clock reset to 14 seconds?

A) After a defensive foul

B) After an offensive foul

C) After an offensive rebound

D) After a shot hits the rim but does not go in

Question 8:

What happens if a player commits a technical foul?

A) The player is immediately ejected

B) The opposing team is awarded one free throw

C) The opposing team is awarded two free throws

D) The game is paused for 5 minutes

Question 9:

Which of the following is not a violation in basketball?

A) Double dribble

B) Carrying

C) Goaltending

D) Substitution

Question 10:

What is the penalty for a flagrant foul?

A) Immediate ejection of the player who committed the foul

B) Two free throws and possession of the ball to the fouled team

C) Technical foul assessed to the coach

D) Loss of one timeout for the team committing the foul

(Solution on page 120)

Game 2 - Spot the Difference: Historic NBA Finals

Welcome to an electrifying game of Spot the Difference! Dive into the world of NBA Finals history and test your attention to detail with two gripping descriptions of a famous game. Your mission? Identify 19 differences in Text B. Get ready for a challenge that will sharpen your mind and ignite your passion for basketball! Let's get started!

Description A

The 1998 NBA Finals were a showdown between the Chicago Bulls and the Utah Jazz. The series went to six games, with the Bulls winning their sixth championship. This series was particularly memorable for the intensity and high level of play displayed by both teams. Each game was a battle of wills, with neither team willing to concede an inch. In Game 6, Michael Jordan delivered one of the most iconic performances of his career. With the Bulls trailing 86-83 in the final minute, Jordan made a crucial layup, reducing the deficit to one point. Moments later, he stole the ball from Karl Malone and dribbled up the court. With 5.2 seconds left, Jordan executed a crossover dribble and hit a 20-foot jumper over Bryon Russell, securing an 87-86 victory for the Bulls. This shot is often referred to as "The Last Shot" and is celebrated as one of the greatest moments in NBA history.

Scottie Pippen, playing through a back injury that had plagued him throughout the series, contributed with 15 points and 8 rebounds. Despite the pain, Pippen's determination and skill were crucial to the Bulls' success. Dennis Rodman, known for his defensive prowess and rebounding skills, added 8 points and 10 rebounds. Rodman's presence in the paint was a significant factor in limiting the Jazz's scoring opportunities. For the Jazz, Karl Malone scored 31 points, showcasing his scoring ability and physical dominance in the post. John Stockton, the Jazz's veteran point guard, had 17 points and 8 assists, orchestrating the offense with precision. Despite their efforts, the Jazz couldn't overcome the Bulls' resilience and tenacity. The series is remembered not only for its thrilling conclusion but also for the high level of competition and the legendary status it cemented for several players involved.

Description B

The 2000 NBA Finals were a showdown between the Chicago Bulls and the Los Angeles Lakers. The series went to seven games, with the Bulls winning their fifth championship. This series was particularly memorable for the controversies and high level of play displayed by both teams. Each game was a battle of wills, with neither team willing to concede an inch. In Game 6, Michael Jordan delivered one of the most iconic performances of his career. With the Bulls trailing 89-86 in the final minute, Jordan made a crucial layup, reducing the deficit to one point. Moments later, he stole the ball from Shaquille O'Neal and dribbled up the court. With 5.2 seconds left, Jordan executed a crossover dribble and hit a 25-foot three-pointer over Kobe Bryant, securing an 89-88 victory for the Bulls. This shot is often referred to as "The Last Shot" and is celebrated as one of the greatest moments in NBA history.

Scottie Pippen, playing through a back injury that had plagued him throughout the series, contributed with 18 points and 9 rebounds. Despite the pain, Pippen's determination and skill were crucial to the Bulls' success. Dennis Rodman, known for his defensive prowess and rebounding skills, added 12 points and 12 rebounds. Rodman's presence in the paint was a significant factor in limiting the Lakers' scoring opportunities. For the Lakers, Karl Malone scored 28 points, showcasing his scoring ability and physical dominance in the post. John Stockton, the Lakers' veteran point guard, had 17 points and 8 assists, orchestrating the offense with precision. Despite their efforts, the Lakers couldn't overcome the Bulls' resilience and tenacity. The series is remembered not only for its thrilling conclusion but also for the high level of competition and the legendary status it cemented for several players involved.

Take your time and enjoy the challenge. When you're ready, check the solution provided below to see how many differences you spotted correctly!

(Solution on page 122)

Game 3 - Basketball Legends Word Search

Welcome to the Basketball Legends Word Search! This is a fun game where you find the names of 12 famous basketball players hidden in a big box of letters. Here's how to play:

Objective:

- Find all 12 names of famous basketball players hidden in the box of letters.

How to Play:

1. **Look for Names:** The names can be hidden in these ways:

   - **Across:** From left to right or from right to left.

   - **Up and Down:** From top to bottom or from bottom to top.

   - **Diagonal:** Slanting in any direction.

2. **Names can Share Letters:** Sometimes names will cross each other and share letters.

3. **Check the List:** There is a list of the 12 names below the box to help you know what to look for.

4. **Mark the Names:** When you find a name, write down where it starts and where it ends.

- For example, If you find the name "JORDAN" starting at the top left and ending at the bottom right, you can write down those positions. Now, let's start finding those basketball legends! Have fun!

Basketball Legends List:

- Dirk Nowitzki, Hakeem Olajuwo, Kevin Durant, Kobe Bryant, Larry Bird, LeBron James, Magic Johnson, Michael Jordan, Shaquille O'Neal, Stephen Curry, Tim Duncan, Wilt Chamberlain

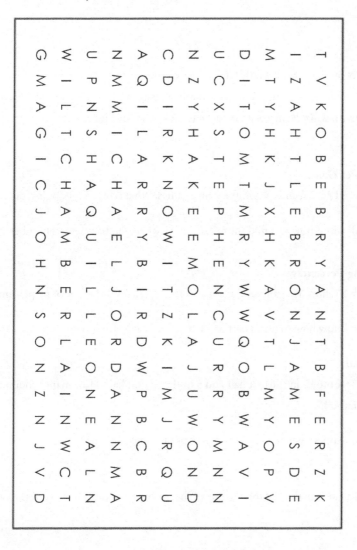

(Solution on page 124)

Game 4 – Basketball Math Challenge

Welcome to the Basketball Math Challenge! Get ready to solve 10 exciting problems related to basketball statistics. Use your math skills to find the answers and become a basketball math whiz! Remember, if you get stuck, read the hint to help you out.

1. Points Per Game

Michael scored 20, 25, and 18 points in three games. What is his average points per game?

Hint: Think about how you find the middle value when you have several numbers.

2. Shooting Percentage

Emma took 15 shots in a game and made 9 of them. What was her shooting percentage?

Hint: If you know how to find a part of a whole, you can solve this.

3. Rebounds

Avery got 7 rebounds in the first half and 5 in the second half. How many rebounds did Avery get in total?

Hint: What happens when you put two groups of things together?

4. Assists

Lucas has 12 assists in the first three games of the season. How many assists does he average per game?

Hint: Sharing fairly among friends might give you an idea.

5. Free Throw Success

Sophia made 16 out of her 20 free throw attempts. What is her free throw percentage?

Hint: It's like turning part of a pizza into a number out of 100.

6. Total Points Scored

Noah scored 10 points in the first quarter, 8 in the second, 12 in the third, and 5 in the fourth. How many points did he score in total?

Hint: Adding up all the pieces will give you the whole.

7. Blocks Per Game

Liam had 3 blocks in one game, 4 in another, and 2 in the next. What is his average number of blocks per game?

Hint: Think about finding the balance point of several numbers.

8. Field Goals Made

Olivia made 7 field goals in the first half and 6 in the second half. How many field goals did she make in total?

Hint: Combining groups is the key here.

9. Steals

Ethan stole the ball 5 times in one game and 3 times in another. How many steals did he make in total?

Hint: Counting all the times together will help.

10. Win Percentage

A team played 30 games and won 18 of them. What is their win percentage?

Hint: Compare the wins to the total games, and then think about the whole divided into 100 parts.

(Solution on page 125)

Game 5 - Basketball Timeline: Evolution of the Game

Welcome to the Basketball Timeline game! Your goal is to put these key events in basketball history in the correct chronological order. By doing so, you'll learn about the major milestones that have shaped the sport into what it is today.

The Dream Team Dominates!

The USA "Dream Team," full of NBA stars, wins the gold medal at the Barcelona Olympics. (Hint: Year the Mall of America opened.)

Basketball Joins the Olympic Party!

Basketball debuts at the Berlin Summer Olympics. The USA wins the first gold medal in basketball. (Hint: Same year as Jesse Owens' triumph.)

The Birth of Basketball Madness!

James Naismith invents basketball in Springfield, Massachusetts, at the International YMCA Training School. (Hint: Near the end of the 19th century.)

The BAA Bounces into Action!

The Basketball Association of America (BAA) is founded. It merges with the National Basketball League (NBL) to form the NBA. (Hint: The year after the end of WWII.)

Wilt's Epic 100-Point Game!

Wilt Chamberlain scores 100 points in a game for the Philadelphia Warriors against the New York Knicks. (Hint: The same year as John Glenn orbited the Earth.)

Celtics Start Their Winning Streak!

The Boston Celtics win their first NBA Championship, beginning their dynasty under coach Red Auerbach and star Bill Russell. (Hint: Around the time Sputnik was launched.)

LeBron James Enters the NBA Scene!

LeBron James joins the NBA with the Cleveland Cavaliers as the number one overall pick in the NBA Draft. (Hint: The year Arnold Schwarzenegger became governor of California.)

The Magic vs. Bird Showdown Begins!

Magic Johnson and Larry Bird bring their rivalry to the NBA, boosting the league's popularity. (Hint: At the end of the disco era.)

The WNBA Takes the Court!

The Women's National Basketball Association (WNBA) is established. (Hint: Year the Summer Olympics returned to the USA.)

The First Professional Hoop Showdown!

In Trenton, New Jersey, the Trenton Basketball Team faces the Brooklyn YMCA in the first known professional basketball game. (Hint: Five years before the turn of the century.)

(Solution on page 128)

Game 6 - Fill-in-the-Blanks

Get ready to test your basketball knowledge with a fun fill-in-the-blanks activity! Perfect for players, fans, or anyone curious about the sport. Each sentence has a blank space for a basketball term. Use your basketball knowledge to complete each sentence. Compare your answers with the solutions at the end.

Final Fill-in-the-Blanks and Solutions

1. The object used to play basketball is called a _____.

2. The player who dribbles and passes the ball is known as the _____ guard.

3. There are _____ players on each basketball team on the court at the same time.

4. The ring where players try to score points is called the _____.

5. A shot is worth _____ if made from inside the three-point line.

6. The _____ line is where players stand to shoot free throws.

7. The player who often plays near the basket and blocks shots is called the _____.

8. A _____ is a pass to a teammate that leads directly to a score.

9. _____ occurs when a player illegally moves their feet without dribbling the ball.

10. _____ happens when a player touches the ball while it is on its way down to the basket.

11. A game of basketball begins with a _____ ball at center court.

12. A _____ is a type of foul where a player makes illegal physical contact with an opponent during play.

13. When a player catches the ball after a missed shot, it is called a _____.

14. The player who often scores from close range and may play near the basket is called _____.

15. A _____ is when a player makes a basket while being fouled and then gets a free throw.

(Solution on page 130)

Game 7 – Pattern Recognition: NBA Draft Picks and Rookie Achievements

Welcome to the NBA Draft Picks Pattern Recognition Challenge! In this game, you'll be presented with sequences involving NBA draft picks and their notable rookie achievements. Your task is to recognize the patterns and complete them. This game will help you sharpen your pattern recognition and memory skills while enhancing your knowledge of NBA draft history. Are you ready to get started? Let's dive in!

Instructions:

1. Carefully read each sequence and identify the pattern.

2. Complete the sequence based on the identified pattern.

3. Use hints if you're stuck, but try to solve as many as you can without them!

Sequences

Sequence 1: Draft Year and Rookie of the Year (ROY) Winners

- 2003: LeBron James

- 2004: Emeka Okafor

- 2005: Chris Paul

- 2006: Brandon Roy

- 2007: Kevin Durant

- 2008: ?

Hint:

Look at the sequence of years and identify the ROY for 2008.

Sequence 2: Draft Position and Rookie Scoring Leaders

- 2009, 1st Pick: Blake Griffin

- 2010, 1st Pick: John Wall

- 2011, 1st Pick: Kyrie Irving

- 2012, 1st Pick: Anthony Davis

- 2013, 1st Pick: Anthony Bennett

- 2014, 1st Pick: ?

Hint:

Identify the player picked first in the 2014 NBA Draft who led rookies in scoring.

Sequence 3: Draft Team and All-Star Selections (First 3 Seasons)

- Chicago Bulls: Michael Jordan (3 All-Star selections)

- Cleveland Cavaliers: LeBron James (2 All-Star selections)

- Philadelphia 76ers: Allen Iverson (3 All-Star selections)

- Los Angeles Lakers: Magic Johnson (2 All-Star selections)

- Minnesota Timberwolves: Kevin Garnett (1 All-Star selection)

- Milwaukee Bucks: ?

Hint:

Identify a Milwaukee Bucks player who had multiple All-Star selections in his first three seasons.

Sequence 4: Rookie Triple-Doubles

- Magic Johnson: 7

- Ben Simmons: 12

- Jason Kidd: 4

- Lamar Odom: 3

- Luka Dončić: 8

- LaMelo Ball: ?

Hint:

Find the number of triple-doubles achieved by LaMelo Ball in his rookie season.

Sequence 5: Draft Year and Rookie Team Wins

- 2011: Cleveland Cavaliers - 19 wins

- 2012: New Orleans Hornets - 21 wins

- 2013: Orlando Magic - 20 wins

- 2014: Philadelphia 76ers - 18 wins

- 2015: Minnesota Timberwolves - 16 wins

- 2016: ?

Hint:

Identify the team and number of wins for the 2016 NBA Draft top pick's team.

(Solution on page 132)

Solutions – Basketball Brain Games And Trivia!

Game 1 – Basketball Rules Trivia Challenge (Solution)

Answers and Explanations

Question 1: Answer: B) 5 seconds
Explanation: According to official basketball rules, an offensive player who is closely guarded must dribble, pass, or shoot within 5 seconds. This rule is intended to maintain the flow of the game and prevent stalling.

Question 2: Answer: C) 6 fouls
Explanation: In the NBA, a player is disqualified after committing 6 personal fouls. However, in high school and college basketball, the limit is 5 personal fouls.

Question 3: Answer: A) Moving your pivot foot after stopping your dribble
Explanation: Traveling occurs when a player moves their pivot foot illegally, which means they have taken too many steps without dribbling the ball.

Question 4: Answer: B) 3 seconds
Explanation: In the NBA, a defensive player is not allowed to stay in the key area for more than 3 seconds without actively guarding an opponent. This is to prevent zone defense abuses.

Question 5: Answer: B) 2 steps
Explanation: After a player stops dribbling, they are allowed to take two steps before they must pass, shoot, or come to a stop.

Question 6: Answer: C) 3 points
Explanation: A basket is worth 3 points if the shooter releases the ball from behind the three-point line.

Question 7: Answer: C) After an offensive rebound
Explanation: In the NBA, if the offense grabs an offensive rebound, the shot clock is reset to 14 seconds instead of the full 24 seconds.

Question 8: Answer: B) The opposing team is awarded one free throw
Explanation: When a player commits a technical foul, the opposing team is awarded one free throw, and play resumes with possession awarded based on the situation before the foul.

Question 9: Answer: D) Substitution
Explanation: Substitution is not a violation; it's a normal part of the game where players are exchanged on the court.

Question 10: Answer: B) Two free throws and possession of the ball to the fouled team
Explanation: A flagrant foul is penalized with two free throws for the fouled team and possession of the ball. Depending on the severity, the player committing the foul may also be ejected.

(Questions on page 103)

Game 2 – Spot the Difference: Historic NBA Finals (Solution)

Ready to see how you did? Here are the 19 differences highlighted in Description B. Check your answers and see how many you managed to spot!

Description B

The **2000** NBA Finals were a showdown between the Chicago Bulls and the **Los Angeles Lakers**. The series went to **seven** games, with the Bulls winning their **fifth** championship. This series was particularly memorable for the **controversies** and high level of play displayed by both teams. Each game was a battle of wills, with neither team willing to concede an inch. In Game 6, Michael Jordan delivered one of the most iconic performances of his career. With the Bulls trailing **89-86** in the final minute, Jordan made a crucial layup, reducing the deficit to one point. Moments later, he stole the ball from **Shaquille O'Neal** and dribbled up the court. With 5.2 seconds left, Jordan executed a crossover dribble and hit a **25-foot three-pointer** over **Kobe Bryant**, securing an **89-88** victory for the Bulls. This shot is often referred to as "The Last Shot" and is celebrated as one of the greatest moments in NBA history.

Scottie Pippen, playing through a back injury that had plagued him throughout the series, contributed with **18** points and **9** rebounds. Despite the pain, Pippen's determination and skill were crucial to the Bulls' success. Dennis Rodman, known for his defensive prowess and rebounding skills, added **12** points and **12** rebounds. Rodman's presence in the paint was a significant factor in limiting the **Lakers'** scoring opportunities. For the **Lakers,** Karl Malone scored **28** points, showcasing his scoring ability and physical dominance in the post. John Stockton, the **Lakers'** veteran point guard, had 17 points and 8 assists, orchestrating the offense with precision. Despite their efforts, the **Lakers** couldn't overcome the Bulls' resilience and tenacity. The series is remembered not only for its thrilling conclusion but also for the high level of competition and the legendary status it cemented for several players involved.

And here are the 19 differences between Description A and Description B, all together: *2000, Los Angeles Lakers, seven, fifth, controversies, 89-86, Shaquille O'Neal, 25-foot three-pointer, Kobe Bryant, 89-88, 18, 9, 12, 12, Lakers, Lakers, 28, Lakers', Lakers*

Great job on completing the Spot the Difference challenge! How many of the 19 differences did you find? Whether you spotted all of them or just a few, you've sharpened your attention to detail. Keep up the great work and enjoy more brain games!

(Questions on page 106)

Game 3 - Basketball Legends Word Search (Solution)

Hey there, puzzle master! Ready to see if your detective skills were on point? The solution is right below, so dive in to find out if you've tracked down all 12 basketball legends hidden in the grid. How many did you find?

```
T  .  K  O  B  E  B  R  Y  A  N  T  .  .  .  .  .  K
I  .  .  .  .  L  E  B  R  O  N  J  A  M  E  S  .  E
M  .  .  .  .  .  .  .  .  .  .  .  .  .  .  .  .  V
D  .  .  .  .  .  .  .  .  .  .  .  .  .  .  .  .  I
U  .  .  S  T  E  P  H  E  N  C  U  R  R  Y  .  .  N
N  .  .  H  A  K  E  E  M  O  L  A  J  U  W  O  N  D
C  D  I  R  K  N  O  W  I  T  Z  K  I  .  .  .  .  U
A  .  .  L  A  R  R  Y  B  I  R  D  .  .  .  .  .  R
N  .  M  I  C  H  A  E  L  J  O  R  D  A  N  .  .  A
.  .  .  S  H  A  Q  U  I  L  L  E  O  N  E  A  L  N
W  I  L  T  C  H  A  M  B  E  R  L  A  I  N  .  .  T
.  M  A  G  I  C  J  O  H  N  S  O  N  .  .  .  .  .
```

(Questions on page 108)

Game 4 – Basketball Math Challenge (Solution)

1. Points Per Game

Michael scored 20, 25, and 18 points in three games. What is his average points per game?

- First, add up all the points: 20 + 25 + 18 = 63

- Then, divide by the number of games: 63 ÷ 3 = 21

- Michael's average points per game is **21**.

2. Shooting Percentage

Emma took 15 shots in a game and made 9 of them. What was her shooting percentage?

- First, divide the number of shots made by the total shots: 9 ÷ 15 = 0.6

- Then, multiply by 100 to get the percentage: 0.6 × 100 = 60%

- Emma's shooting percentage is **60%**.

3. Rebounds

Avery got 7 rebounds in the first half and 5 in the second half. How many rebounds did Avery get in total?

- Add the rebounds from both halves: 7 + 5 = 12

- Avery got a total of **12 rebounds**.

4. Assists

Lucas has 12 assists in the first three games of the season. How many assists does he average per game?

- Divide the total assists by the number of games: 12 ÷ 3 = 4

- Lucas averages **4 assists** per game.

5. Free Throw Success

Sophia made 16 out of her 20 free throw attempts. What is her free throw percentage?

- First, divide the number of successful free throws by the total attempts: 16 ÷ 20 = 0.8

- Then, multiply by 100 to get the percentage: 0.8 × 100 = 80%

- Sophia's free throw percentage is **80%**.

6. Total Points Scored

Noah scored 10 points in the first quarter, 8 in the second, 12 in the third, and 5 in the fourth. How many points did he score in total?

- Add up all the points from each quarter: 10 + 8 + 12 + 5 = 35

- Noah scored a total of **35 points**.

7. Blocks Per Game

Liam had 3 blocks in one game, 4 in another, and 2 in the next. What is his average number of blocks per game?

- First, add up all the blocks: 3 + 4 + 2 = 9

- Then, divide by the number of games: 9 ÷ 3 = 3

- Liam averages **3 blocks** per game.

8. Field Goals Made

Olivia made 7 field goals in the first half and 6 in the second half. How many field goals did she make in total?

- Add the field goals from both halves: 7 + 6 = 13

- Olivia made a total of **13 field goals**.

9. Steals

Ethan stole the ball 5 times in one game and 3 times in another. How many steals did he make in total?

- Add the steals from both games: 5 + 3 = 8

- Ethan made a total of **8 steals**.

10. Win Percentage

A team played 30 games and won 18 of them. What is their win percentage?

- First, divide the number of wins by the total number of games: 18 ÷ 30 = 0.6

- Then, multiply by 100 to get the percentage: 0.6 × 100 = 60%

- The team's win percentage is **60%**.

Enjoy solving these basketball math problems, and keep practicing to improve both your math and basketball skills!

(Questions on page 110)

Game 5 - Basketball Timeline (Solution)

1891: The Birth of Basketball Madness!

James Naismith, a genius with a wild imagination, invents basketball in Springfield, Massachusetts, while working at the International YMCA Training School. Picture this: a soccer ball and peach baskets as the first hoops!

1896: The First Professional Hoop Showdown!

In Trenton, New Jersey, the Trenton Basketball Team faces off against the Brooklyn YMCA in the first known professional basketball game. Imagine the excitement as they dribble and shoot like pros for the first time ever!

1936: Basketball Joins the Olympic Party!

Basketball makes its grand entrance at the Berlin Summer Olympics. The USA, showing off their mad skills, snags the first gold medal in basketball. High-fives all around!

1946: The BAA Bounces into Action!

The Basketball Association of America (BAA) is born. Just a few years later, in 1949, it teams up with the National Basketball League (NBL) to create the ultimate league we know today as the NBA!

1957: Celtics Start Their Winning Streak!

The Celtics capture their first NBA Championship, kicking off an epic dynasty under the legendary coach Red Auerbach and superstar Bill Russell. Talk about a slam dunk!

1962: Wilt's Epic 100-Point Game!

On March 2, 1962, Wilt Chamberlain pulls off the unthinkable, scoring a jaw-dropping 100 points in a single game for the Philadelphia Warriors against the New York Knicks. That's a whole lot of buckets!

1979-1980: The Magic vs. Bird Showdown Begins!

Magic Johnson and Larry Bird take their college rivalry to the NBA, turning every game into must-watch TV and skyrocketing the league's popularity. Their epic battles start in the 1979-1980 season. Grab your popcorn!

1992: The Dream Team Dominates!

The USA "Dream Team," packed with NBA superstars, dazzles the world at the Barcelona Olympics, easily grabbing the gold medal and showing everyone just how awesome NBA players really are.

1996: The WNBA Takes the Court!

The Women's National Basketball Association (WNBA) is launched, giving amazing female athletes their own league. The first season tips off in 1997, and girl power takes over the court!

2003: LeBron James Enters the NBA Scene!

LeBron James, the teenage phenom, joins the NBA with the Cleveland Cavaliers as the number one overall pick in the 2003 NBA Draft. The world better get ready for some King James magic!

(Questions on page 112)

Game 6 - Game 6 - Fill-in-the-Blanks (Solution)

Great job completing the Basketball Fill-in-the-Blanks game! Now, let's see how well you did. Below are the full phrases, with the missing words highlighted in. Check your answers and see how much you've learned about basketball :D

1. The object used to play basketball is called a **basketball.**

2. The player who dribbles and passes the ball is known as the **point** guard.

3. There are **five** players on each basketball team on the court at the same time.

4. The ring where players try to score points is called the **hoop**.

5. A shot is worth **two points** if made from inside the three-point line.

6. The **free-throw** line is where players stand to shoot free throws.

7. The player who often plays near the basket and blocks shots is called the **center**.

8. An **assist** is a pass to a teammate that leads directly to a score.

9. **Traveling** occurs when a player illegally moves their feet without dribbling the ball.

10. **Goaltending** happens when a player touches the ball while it is on its way down to the basket.

11. A game of basketball begins with a **jump ball** at center court.

12. A **personal foul** is a type of foul where a player makes illegal physical contact with an opponent during play.

13. When a player catches the ball after a missed shot, it is called a **rebound**.

14. The player who often scores from close range and may play near the basket is called the **center** (also **Power forward**).

15. A **three-point play** is when a player makes a basket while being fouled and then gets a free throw.

(Questions on page 114)

Game 7 – Pattern Recognition: NBA Draft Picks and Rookie Achievements (Solution)

Get ready to slam dunk the solutions! Here are the answers to the NBA Draft Picks Pattern Recognition Challenge. Each sequence is now complete with the correct historical data and patterns. Let's see if your guesses matched up with the actual stats—time to celebrate those rookie achievements!

Solution 1: Draft Year and ROY Winners

- 2008: Derrick Rose

Solution 2: Draft Position and Rookie Scoring Leaders

- 2014, 1st Pick: Andrew Wiggins

Solution 3: Draft Team and All-Star Selections (First 3 Seasons)

- Milwaukee Bucks: Kareem Abdul-Jabbar (3 All-Star selections)

Solution 4: Rookie Triple-Doubles

- LaMelo Ball: 6

Solution 5: Draft Year and Rookie Team Wins

- 2016: Philadelphia 76ers - 28 wins

(Questions on page 116)

Afterword

Hey, hoop heroes! We've hit the final buzzer of our basketball journey. From Michael Jordan's soaring dunks to Kareem Abdul-Jabbar's records, and Shaquille O'Neal's dominance, we've explored legendary players who shaped the game. We laughed at epic blunders and marveled at moments like Wilt Chamberlain's 100-point game and LeBron James' chase-down blocks. You tackled brain-busting games and trivia, showing your basketball smarts.

So, what's next, future star? Will you break records, coach a team, or invent the next big thing in basketball? Remember to practice hard, stay determined, and always play with passion.

If you enjoyed this book, I'd love to hear your thoughts, just _**scan**_ the QR code below and leave a review. Tell me what chapter did you like, or what do you want my next book to be; and I promise I read every single one!

Psst... Want to see more books I've written? _**scan**_ the QR code below to find my Amazon page!

See you on the court, future legend! Harris

Made in the USA
Monee, IL
17 December 2024

74156860R00079